Language and Legal Proceedings

Endurence Midinette Koumassol Dissake

Language and Legal Proceedings

Analysing Courtroom Discourse in Cameroon

palgrave
macmillan

Endurence Midinette Koumassol Dissake
Buea, Cameroon

ISBN 978-3-030-76348-0   ISBN 978-3-030-76349-7 (eBook)
https://doi.org/10.1007/978-3-030-76349-7

This Palgrave Macmillan imprint is published by the registered company Springer Nature Switzerland AG.
The registered company address is: Gewerbestrasse 11, 6330 Cham, Switzerland

Foreword

This book undertakes a linguistic analysis of the discourse of court proceedings in order to determine communication problems in the process of interaction between legal experts (judges, state counsels, and lawyers) and non-legal experts (plaintiff, accused, and witness), as a verification of the efficacy of the implementation of Cameron's language policy of official English-French bilingualism over a background of a de facto national language multilingualism. The book is a landmark endeavour in the use of Discourse Analysis and ideas from Forensic Linguistics to mirror the language problems of courtroom drama in a multilingual setting and their real or potential negative impact on the justice system.

The *Qualitative Method* is motivated, rationalised, and used for the research along with an eclectic combination of two data elicitation procedures (*non-participant observation* of court sessions and *semi-structured interview* of legal experts). The 'Discourse Analysis' framework is chosen as the most appropriate theory for the type of data to be analysed in the research; more specifically, the model of the *Speech Act Theory* of Austin (1962) amplified, inter alia, by Searle (1969) and others is used along with an occasional recourse to the interactional sociolinguistic model of Gumperz (1982).

The presentation and analysis of discourse from courtroom sessions of magistrate courts show that with respect to norms of the speech act theory, non-legal expert participants in the court sessions exhibit enormous communication difficulties evident in the violation of Austin's Felicity Conditions (conventionality and actuality conditions). On the other hand, legal experts seek to rectify these violations through illocutionary acts (exercitives, verdictives, behabitives, and receptive). Specifically, most lay-litigants have two categories of language problems: those resulting from the use of the official languages (English and French) for which they have inadequate competence and those emanating from the use of the legal jargon.

Professional Court interpreters are needed for the vast majority of participants (accused, plaintiffs, and witnesses) who speak essentially or only a Cameroon national language (including Pidgin English) and those whose knowledge of the official languages is functionally inadequate. In the absence of legal provision for a corps of court interpreters, discretional use of untrained amateur (unsworn) interpreters further aggravate and compromise the validity of *due process* in the courtroom drama. The work further reveals that legal experts may be knowledgeable with respect to the law, but their legal training does not prepare them to face the complex language-related and language-dependent problems of court sessions in a multilingual judiciary system.

In addition to advocacy for the formal use of neglected indigenous languages in partnership with the official languages of English and French and a corps of trained interpreters, some suggestions are provided with respect to the use of Forensic Linguistic considerations to solve the identified legal language-related problems. The findings lend credence to our advocacy for a comprehensive language law or language charters for multilingual nations of Africa and beyond (Chumbow 2013 "Towards a legal framework for language Charters in Africa"). Such a language law makes legal provisions for planned, efficient, and effective use of all languages of the nation in the service of education, social integration, social inclusion, and social justice in the enterprise of pluralism and participatory sustainable development.

Emeritus Professor of Linguistics, University of Yaoundé President of the Assembly of Academicians, African Academy of Languages, African Union

Beban Sammy Chumbow

Acknowledgements

I am deeply indebted to Prof. Gratien G. Atindogbé of the University of Buea in Cameroon, who read and commented in detail on every chapter of this dissertation. My profound gratitude goes to Prof. Dr Eric Achimbe of the University of Bayreuth in Germany, who helped to define the scope of this research work.

The data presented and analysed were collected in Cameroon Courts of First Instances for three years. I wish to thank all those court participants, both legal and non-legal practitioners, who provided rich data for this work. Particular thanks go to those legal practitioners (judges, state counsels, lawyers, and interpreters) who received me and answered my questions.

Contents

Abbreviations and Conventions

Court Participants

AC	Accused person
CK/GR	Clerk
DL/AD	Defence lawyer
IN	Interpreter
J	Judge
O	Other participant
PL	Plaintiff
PRW/AP	Prosecution witness
PW/TP	Plaintiff-witness
SC/PR	State council

Concepts and Institutions

ASM	American Sign Language
CSL	Cameroon Sign Language
DA	Discourse Analysis
EJTN	Electro-Static Detection Apparatus
ESDA	European Judicial Training Network
FL	Forensic Linguistics
FLS	Forensic Linguistic Studies
IS	Interactional Sociolinguistics
JD	Jurist Degree
L1	First Language

L2	Second Language
LADO	Language Analysis and Determination of Origin
PACE	Police and Criminal Evidence Art
SAT	Speech Act Theory
UE	European Union
UN	United Nation
UNESCO	United Nations Educational, Scientific and Cultural Organization

Transcription Conventions

(...)	Non-ethical utterances
↑	Tone rising
↓	Tone lowering
[...]	Irrelevant utterances
(.)	Silence
(^^^)	Laughter
< >	English translation
/ /	Author explanations
// //	Words said at the same time
...	Utterance interrupted
{}	Signed utterances

List of Figures

List of Tables

CHAPTER 1

Introduction

The central argument in this book is that the implementation of a non-inclusive language policy in courtrooms brings in serious legal language-related problems. Indeed, languages barrier in courtrooms hinders fair hearings and trials. The language problems of Cameroon courtrooms call for linguistic solutions (Forensic linguistics). But before getting into the solutions, we need to (1) understand the legal system and the language policy of Cameroon, (2) review relevant literature on Forensic Linguistic studies, (3) describe and analyse Cameroon courtroom discourse, and (4) examine legal authorities' attitude towards Cameroon legal language-related problems.

Chapter 2 provides a detailed description of the legal system and the language policy of Cameroon. Cameroon has a bijural system of law (Common and Civil law) and a bilingual language policy (English and French). It is generally said that Cameroon owes its legal and linguistics status to its ancient colonial masters; thus, the current legal system and language policy of Cameroon are vestiges of the colonial past. Actually, Cameroon went through two colonial experiences: the German protectorate period, from 1884 to 1916, and the combined British and French mandatory agreement, from 1916 to 1961. After Cameroon got its independence, in 1961, two major decisions were taken. First, it was decided that English and French will be the official languages of the 'Federal Republic of Cameroon' today known as the 'Republic of Cameroon'. Second, two legal systems will be implemented in Cameroon, the Common

E. M. K. Dissake, *Language and Legal Proceedings*,
https://doi.org/10.1007/978-3-030-76349-7_1

and the Civil laws. Therefore, Cameroon will have a bijural legal system. However, from the early 1970s till today, the legal system of Cameroon has transformed. The bijural legal system has changed in such a way that we can neither identify the Common or Civil law systems. In fact, the translocation of the Common law and the Civil law to Cameroon earlier last century has created differences between the legal traditions of England and France where they originated. Today, modern Cameroon legal system is a hybrid, a modified version of the received laws, peculiarly adapted to its environment, that is, local (customary laws) and imported laws, and international treaties, harmonised and integrated.

There are eight court systems in Cameroon, but I limited the research scope to the Court of First Instance. Courts of First Instance are governed by sections 13, 14, and 15 of *law No 2006/015 of 29 December 2006* on Judicial organisation. According to section 13 of this law, the Court of First Instance is found in every sub-division. Section 14 lays down the composition of the Court of First Instance; at the bench, there is a president, one or more magistrates, one registrar in chief, and one or more registrars. At the preliminary inquiry, there are one or more examining magistrates, one or more registrars. At the legal department, a judicial officer hearing and determining all cases brought to the court. Section 15 lays down the court's jurisdiction to hear civil, criminal, and labour matters and also tries simple offences and related misdemeanours with damages of fine charged not more than 10,000,000 frs.

The language policy and the legal system of Cameroon have two things in common: English and French. These languages are the official languages of Cameroon. All legal documents are written in English and French, and courtrooms discourse are conducted either in English or in French, depending on the legal district. Yet, apart from English and French, Cameroon has more than 250 national languages. Indeed, Cameroon is a multilingual nation having two official languages and many national languages. Cameroon national languages belong to three of the four language phyla of Africa (the Afro-Asiatic, Nilo-Saharan, and Niger-Kordofanian phyla). The exclusion of Cameroon national languages from the legal scene has given birth to serious communication problems during court proceedings. The exchange between lay-litigants and legal authorities is effortful. Even if, the law prescribes the presence of interpreters to assist lay-litigants who cannot communicate in English or in French, those interpreters are rarely present in courtrooms because the litigants cannot afford one, and the court authorities hardly provide one. And when circumstances are such that the court authorities have no other choice than to provide an interpreter, the communication problems are still not solved. Indeed, court interpreters are not trained. They are rather volunteers selected on the spot, or from the street.

Legal language-related problems are identified, analysed, and solved under the realm of Forensic Linguistics. Indeed, through Forensic Linguistic studies, scholars developed approaches to analysed courtroom discourse. Therefore, to better analyse the Cameroon context, it is necessary to review the relevant literature. Chapter 3 reviews Forensic linguistic studies related to the areas of discourse analysis (DA), legal language, lay-litigants language proficiency, and multilingualism in the legal context. It is also important to note that despite the evolution of Forensic Linguistics, it is still unknown to many Cameroonians and Africans linguists. Although Forensic Linguistics has become a well-established field of study, it is still absent in several African nations. Indeed, the literature on forensic linguistic studies focuses on the legal language problems of developed nations, the African setting is still very absent from the literature. For instance, Coulthard and Johnson (2010), Drew (1992), and Matoesian (2008) analysed the courtroom discourse of England; Shuy (2001a, b, 2002a, b, 2006), and Cotterill (2002a, b) studied the legal language-related problems of the American courtrooms; Groot (2003) described the aspect of language and law of the Netherland courtrooms; Eades (2012) studied the case of Australia. And He and Feng (2016) analysed the discourse of Chinese courtrooms. In fact, the literature review allows me to argue that the analysis of Cameroon courtroom discourse, in Chap. 4, brings in a new dynamic to the overall domain of discourse analysis in Forensic Linguistic studies.

From 2016 to 2019, I collected courtroom discourse in the Courts of First Instance of Yaoundé, Douala, Bafoussam, Ngaoundéré (Civil law districts), and Buea (a Common law district). I opted to follow the qualitative research method. Dornyei (2007) suggested that the aim and objective of qualitative research are to describe, analyse, and define human behaviours. Actually, I aim to describe and analyse the speech acts of legal professionals and litigants during trials. Cameroon courtroom discourse is still an untouched area of study. Wilkinson and Birmingham (2003) indicated that the qualitative approach is an effective way of exploring new and untouched areas of study.

I used the non-participant observation as an instrument of data collection in courtrooms. Non-participant observation, as define by Kumar

(2011), allows the researcher to witness an event without taking part in the activity of the event. Thus, I was present in courtrooms, but I did not participate in the debates since the focus was on legal professionals' questions and lay-litigants' answers. To note down the court discourse, I used an observation guide. The guide was divided into four: introductory information, court discourse, participant description, and researcher comments.

The courtroom discourse was analysed via the overall framework of Discourse Analysis (DA) as defined in Eggins and Slade (1997). The main DA approach used was the Speech Act Theory (SAT). However, at a certain point of the analysis, a snippet of the Interactional Sociolinguistics (IS) theory was used. Austin (1962) divided the speech act into two categories, the Constatives and the Performatives. The Performatives were further divided into three acts: locutionary, illocutionary, and perlocutionary. Within the performative category, we also have the Felicity conditions. I used the illocutionary acts and the Felicity conditions to analyse legal professionals and lay-litigants speech acts.

First, the illocutionary act. Austin (1962) and Searle (1969) came up with five categories of illocutionary acts: verdictives, exercitives, commissives, behabitives, and expositives. Court authorities like lawyers, state counsels, and judges use illocutionary acts when addressing litigants. For instance, lawyers and state counsels uttered behabitives speech acts to denounce misconduct in court. Judges uttered exercitives speech acts to condemn transgressions, and verdictives speeches to sentence litigants. However, I observed another form of illocutionary acts used by Cameroon legal professionals, but this form has not yet been defined in the literature. Because of illiteracy, many litigants hardly understand English and/or French utterances. Though the law prohibits court members from interpreting from one language to another during trials, I observed court members interpreting from English to Pidgin English to help lay-litigants understand and respond to questions. In my analysis, I called this form of illocutionary act, the receptive illocutionary act. Therefore, the analysis of Cameroon courtroom discourse allowed me to add a sixth illocutionary category to the five already developed by Austin (1962) and Searle (1969).

Literature has rarely highlighted the receptive attitude of legal professionals during courtroom discourse. For instance, Bhatia (2017) and Chaemsaithong (2012) demonstrated that legal stakeholders never tried to make their words to ordinary citizens understandable. Legal texts are written in a highly nominal style rather than verbal style. Eades (2012) analysis of Australian courtroom discourse exposed ways legal professional's language ideologies constrain witnesses. And He and Feng (2016) analysis of Chinese courtrooms discourse proof that legal professional often uses challenging legal discourse to defeat litigants. Therefore, I argue that receptive illocutionary acts are used in cases of a flagrant language barrier. In other words, legal professional utter receptive illocutionary act to break the language barrier that prevents the litigant from answering the examiner questions.

Second, Felicity conditions. These are conditions necessary for the success of speech events. Etsuko (2006) outlined three Felicity conditions: conventionality, actuality, and intentionality. The analysis of Cameroon courtroom discourse highlights the violation of two Felicity conditions (conventionality and actuality conditions) by lay-litigants. However, I noted that these violations were not dilatory tactics, but rather expressions of language inability. Indeed, lay-litigants violated the conventionality condition when answering legal professional questions in their first languages (national languages), and the actuality condition when misinterpreting words or sentences. Therefore, the absence of Cameroon national languages and lingua-franca in courtrooms hinders fair trials and hearings.

Chapter 5, through the analysis of the interviews administered to the legal authorities, explains the attitude of the latter towards the lay-litigant's linguistic weaknesses. Two interview guides were constructed, both were semi-structured interviews. The first interview guide was translated in the two official languages and administered to legal authorities. The interview guide was structured as such: (1) Introduction, (2) training, (3) practice, (4) attitude, and (5) suggestions. The questions moved from general inquiries to specific questions. The second interview guide was in the French language and was administered to the interpreter of the Ngaoundéré Court of First Instance. This interview guide was made up of nine questions, all related to the competence of the interpreter. The guide was only in the French language because it was administered in a Civil law district, Ngaoundéré.

I interviewed a total of 15 legal practitioners, among which 5 Bench Magistrates (judges), 4 state counsels, 5 lawyers, and 1 interpreter. The interviews revealed that Forensic Linguistic studies are still unfamiliar to Cameroon legal authorities. Though they were to be confronted with legal language-related problems daily, they were not prepared to deal with such problems. Indeed, lay-litigant's languages barriers are overlooked by the judicial system of Cameroon. For instance, lay-litigants rarely appreciate the services of interpreters. And when the interpreters are present, their presence never changes anything since they are not trained. The interpreter of the Court of First Instance of Ngaoundéré was not trained to work as a court interpreter.

The last chapter, Chap. 6, concludes the study. The analysis of the courtroom discourse and the interview of legal authorities disclosed the language problems of Cameroon courtrooms (the non-inclusive language policy, the legal jargon, the disregard of languages barriers, and the illiteracy of litigants). All judicial proceedings are written and conducted in English and/or in French. Yet, 40% of the Cameroon population is not literate in those languages (Essono, 2001), but is rather competent in the national languages. In fact, national languages need to be introduced in Cameroon courtrooms. Other linguistic solutions that need consideration is the simplification of the legal jargon; the assessment of litigant's real language proficiencies; and the effective training of court interpreters. Though this study outlines the language problems of Cameroon courtrooms, language issues are not limited to courtrooms. Many realms of the legal system of Cameroon are awaiting description. For example, police interviews, state counsels' investigations, lawyers and client's discourse, court interpretation and translation. However, through this first attempt, I hope to have acquainted the readers on the linguistic conditions of the legal system of Cameroon. And most importantly, I hope that this study will prompt other African linguists to investigate the linguistic situation of their legal systems.

References

Austin, J. L. (1962). *How to do things with words.* Oxford University Press.

Bhatia, V. K. (2017). Interpreting law in socio-pragmatic space. *Semiotica, 2017*(216), 109–130.

Chaemsaithong, K. (2012). Performing self on the witness stand: Stance and relational work in expert witness testimony. *Discourse & Society, 23*(5), 465–486.

Cotterill, J. (2002a). 'Just one more time…': Aspects of intertextuality in the trials of O. J. Simpson. In J. Cotterill (Ed.), *Language in the legal process* (pp. 147–161). Palgrave Macmillan.

Cotterill, J. (2002b). *Language in the legal process.* Palgrave Macmillan.

Coulthard, M., & Johnson, A. (2010). *The Routledge handbook of forensic linguistics.* Routledge.

Dornyei, Z. (2007). *Research methods in applied linguistics: Quantitative, qualitative and mixed methodologies.* Oxford University Press.

Drew, P. (1992). Contested evidence in courtroom cross-examination: The case of a trial for rape. In P. Drew & J. Heritage (Eds.), *Talk at work* (pp. 470–520). Cambridge University Press.

Eades, D. (2012). The social consequences of language ideologies in courtroom cross-examination. *Language in Society, 41*(4), 471–497.

Eggins, S., & Slade, D. (1997). *Analysing casual conversation*. Cassell.

Essono, J.-M. (2001). Le Cameroun et ses langues. In J.-M. Essono (Ed.), *Cameroun: Politique, langues, économie et santé* (pp. 61–87). L'Harmattan.

Etsuko, O. (2006). Austin's speech act theory and the speech situation. *Esercizi Filosofici, 1*, 1–14.

Groot, G. R. (2003). *Language and law*. Maastricht University Press.

He, X., & Feng, Y. (2016). Mismatched discourses in the petition of Chinese courts. *Law & Social Inquiry, 41*(1), 212–241.

Kumar, R. (2011). *Research methodology: A step by step guide for beginners* (3rd ed.). Sage.

Matoesian, G. M. (2008). You might win the battle but lose the war: Multimodal, interactive, and extralinguistic aspects of witness resistance. *Journal of English Linguistics, 36*(3), 195–218.

Searle, J. (1969). *Speech acts: An essay in the philosophy of language*. Cambridge University Press.

Shuy, W. R. (2001a). DARE's role in linguistic profiling. *Dictionary of American Regional English Newsletter*, 00–10. Retrieved from https://dare.wisc.edu/dare-newsletters/

Shuy, W. R. (2001b). Discourse analysis in the legal context. In D. Schiffrin, D. Tannen, & H. Hamilton (Eds.), *The handbook of discourse analysis* (pp. 437–452). Blackwell.

Shuy, W. R. (2002a). Breaking into language and the law: The trial of the insider linguist. In E. J. Alatis, E. H. Hamilton, & A.-H. Tan (Eds.), *Linguistics, language, and the professions: Education, journalism, law, medicine, and technology* (pp. 67–80). Georgetown University Press.

Shuy, W. R. (2002b). To testify or not to testify. In J. Cotterill (Ed.), *Language in the legal process* (pp. 03–18). Palgrave Macmillan.

Shuy, W. R. (2006). *Linguistics in the courtroom: A practical guide*. Oxford University Press.

Wilkinson, D., & Birmingham, P. (2003). *Using research instruments: A guide for researchers*. Routledge.

CHAPTER 2

The Legal System and Language Policy of Cameroon

Introduction

That which must be obeyed and followed by citizens, subject to sanctions or legal consequences, is a law (Garner & Black, 2009), and a system of communication used by a particular country or community, is a language. The legal and linguistic heterogeneity of Cameroon makes the nation a relevant case study. Cameroon is commonly described as 'Africa in miniature' to allude to the fact that the country has a small share of all other African nations. For instance, Cameroon national languages (more than 250) belong to three of the four language phyla of Africa; the two most prominent legal systems in Africa (the Common and the Civil laws) are used in Cameroon; and the two most widespread exoglossic languages (English and French) are spoken in Cameroon. Indeed, Cameroon has a Bijural legal system and an official Bilingualism policy. Studies revealed that Cameroon owes its legal and linguistics status to its ancient colonial masters, in other words, the current legal system and language policy of Cameroon are vestiges of the colonial past. This chapter traces the pre- and post-colonial history of Cameroon. The objective is to describe the linguistic and legal status of Cameroon to properly analyse the observed legal language-related problems of courtrooms.

E. M. K. Dissake, *Language and Legal Proceedings*,
https://doi.org/10.1007/978-3-030-76349-7_2

The Colonial History of Cameroon

Cameroon went through two main colonial experiences: the German protectorate period, from 1884 to 1916, and the combined British and French mandatory agreement, from 1916 to 1961. However, in the 1500s, the Portuguese were the first to show interest in the Cameroon territory. Indeed, the name 'Cameroon' came from the appellation 'Rio dos Camarões' (Shrimp River), a name given by a Portuguese sailor called Fernando Po. Despite being the first to venture into Cameroon, the Portuguese became reluctant to annex the land because of the malaria pandemic in the area. Notwithstanding these challenges, the Germans signed a protectorate agreement with the chiefs of the Wouri estuary, a setting located in the littoral region of Cameroon. This explains why historians argue that the Cameroon of today is mainly a creation of the Germans (Fombad, 2015).

During their colonial era, the Germans managed the cultural and linguistic heterogeneity of Kamerun[1] by administering the territory as a single cohesive modern polity through the Reichstag law of 1886, which conferred powers on the Kaiser to legislate by decree of order and good government. Because of the presence of Germans in Kamerun, the legislation established two court systems: the *Consular Jurisdiction Law* of April 7, 1900, for the Germans, and the *Colonial Law* of September 10, 1900, for Kamerunians native (Fombad, 2015, p. 102). The Consular Jurisdiction law applied European rules and principles in settling German disputes in courts, while the Colonial law applied customary rules and principles in settling Kamerunian disputes. This event marked the coexistence of two different legal systems in Cameroon. Thus, Germans were the first to establish a kind of bijural legal system in the territory. Nonetheless, these two systems were not equal in value. The *Consular Jurisdiction* law had the power of censorship over the *Colonial law*. Indeed, every decision taken by the Colonial legal administrators was sent to the Consular Jurisdiction law for verification, and those decisions were either rejected or reformulated.

German colonial sovereignty lasted for 32 years. After the Second World War (WWII), when German troops were defeated by the combined French and British expeditionary force in Mora in February 1916, the

[1] During the German period, Cameroon was known as Kamerun. Hence, when referring to the German colonial era, Cameron will be written as Kamerun.

Germans signed the Versailles Treaty, where they renounced their rights over their colonial territories. This was followed by the signing of the Anglo-French declaration of July 10, 1919, in Paris which ceded the territory of Cameroon to Britain and France (Rudin, 1938). As such, the country was partitioned by these two conquerors—20% of the territory was taken by the British and the remaining 80% was taken by the French. History does not provide a clear reason why Britain took just 20% of the territory, but many historians speculated that 'the British feared incurring further financial responsibilities in taking on another colonial territory and desired to take on nothing more than what was necessary to consolidate their Nigerian colony' (Fombad, 2015, p. 102). Articles 22 and 23 of the League of Nations Mandated Agreement conferred Britain and France power over Cameroon and article 9 of that same agreement explicitly gave them 'full powers of administration and legislation' and the 'liberty to apply [their] ... laws to the territory under mandate subject to the modifications required by local conditions' (Fombad, 2015, p. 102). This provision marked the starting point of the exportation of the English Common law and French Civil law to Cameroon as well as their languages, English and French.

Just like the Germans, Britain applied two legal systems in its two portions of Cameroon: one implemented in the urban sector and the other implemented in the rural sector. Still, like the Germans, these legal systems were not of equal status. The legal system of the urban sector was superior and had a power of censorship over the rural sector. The urban legal system was administered by British officials who had the power to decide whether or not decisions taken by rural administrators were 'repugnant' and subjected to revision. But, the French way of administering their Cameroon territory was different from the British. The French decree of May 22, 1922, explicitly stated that all laws and decrees promulgated in France had to be extended in their colonial territory. As such, the French Civil law was introduced in Cameroon (Anyangwe, 1987). However, the French also implemented two legal systems in the country—the *justice de droit Française* for the French settling in Cameroon and assimilated Cameroonians (*citoyen*), and the *justice de droit indigène* for Cameroonian indigenes (*sujet*) (Gardinier, 1963, p. 10). These two legal systems were not equal in status. The *justice de droit Français* exercised power over the *justice de droit indigène*. The reign of Britain and France ended in the 1960s.

Forty-five years after Britain and France signed the Anglo-French declaration, they both had to give Cameroon independence. France was the first to do so in 1960 by declaring French Cameroon independent. The French territory was renamed '*La Republique du Cameroun*'. Even though Britain declared Nigeria independent in the same year, Southern and Northern Cameroons administered as an integral part of Nigeria had not yet had their independence; they first had to take an important decision. They had to decide whether they wanted to have their independence under Nigeria or Cameroon. In this light, a referendum was organised, and Northern Cameroon decided to join Nigeria while Southern Cameroon decided to reunify with Cameroon. To properly reunify Southern Cameroon and *la Republique du Cameroun*, it was necessary to recognise that during the colonial period the two territories acquired new cultures, languages, and laws. Therefore, officials had to design an agreement that will satisfy both parties. As such, two major decisions were taken: the first one was about the official languages of the unified nation. It was agreed that the two official languages of the 'Federal Republic of Cameroon', now known as the 'Republic of Cameroon', will be English and French. The second issue concerned the legal system, authorities decided that Southern Cameroon will retain the Common law left by the British, and *La Republique du Cameroun* will maintain the Civil law left by the French; thus, Cameroon will have a Bijural legal system. As demonstrated in Chaps. 3 and 4, the rich colonial history of Cameroon contributed to the birth of legal language-related problems.

The Legal System of Cameroon

The primary component of the Cameroon legal system is bijuralism, that is, the Combination of the Common and Civil laws. The Common law is implemented in the two anglophones regions, the South-West and the North-West, and the Civil law in the eight francophones regions, the Littoral, Centre, East, South, North, Adamawa, Extreme-North, and West.

The English Common law is described as a system that operates on the basis of *Precedence*, that is judges tried cases on the premises of earlier comparable cases. Indeed, in the Common law tradition, judges' decisions become established rules and regulations. However, the French Civil law key distinguishing feature is its *codified* system of law (Dame, 2015, p. 20), putting emphasis on the primacy of written laws, rather than precedent judicial resolutions. The Civil law tradition follows written and codified laws which are the primary sources of law (Apprendre le droit, 2017).

The translocation of the Common law and the Civil law to Cameroon earlier last century has created differences between the legal traditions of England and France where they originated and that of Cameroon into which they were imported. Today, modern Cameroon legal system is a hybrid, indeed a modified version of the received laws, peculiarly adapted to its environment. Moreover, it is, also a novel blend of local (customary laws) and imported laws and international treaties, harmonised and integrated. In other words, we are witnessing the emergence of a new species of Common and Civil laws, a specifically Cameroonian Common/Civil law defined, fortified, and elaborated by local legislation and decisions of courts.

The hybridity of the legal system of Cameroon is a consequence of its customary laws. Many legal experts sustain that to say that Cameroon is a bijural system is a misnomer. Indeed, Customary Law is both a source and a form of law in Cameroon. The Customary courts' ordinance cap 142 of 1948 applicable to Anglophone Cameroon defines customary law as 'the native law and custom prevailing in the area of the jurisdiction of the court so far as it is not repugnant to natural justice, equity and good conscience, nor incompatible either directly or by natural implication with the written law for the time being in force'. However, that Cameroon is a bijural system may yet stand for, the application of customary law in Cameroon is limited. Customary law governs only matters of personal status: customary marriages, divorce, custody, inheritance, adoption, and affiliation and also lands held by customary communities, subject to the provisions of the land decrees of 1974 and 1976. But it may be noted that traditional courts in the villages (i.e. non-statutory courts) exercise jurisdiction over whatever matter, issue, cause, or dispute arising in the village whether civil or criminal. The Cameroon judicial system counts many types of courts.

Ordinance No 72/04 of 26 August 1972 on Judicial Organisation modified by *law No 2006/015 of 29 December 2006* on Judicial organisation classified the courts into two groups. First, the trial courts composed of customary courts, Court of First Instance, high court, military court, and the lower courts of administration. Second, the appellate courts composed of the court of appeal and the supreme court. Because this work is the first attempt to study the legal language-related problems of Cameroon courts, we limited our scope to the Courts of First Instance.

Courts of First Instance are governed by sections 13, 14, and 15 of *law No 2006/015 of 29 December 2006* on Judicial organisation. According to section 13 of this law, the Court of First Instance is found in every sub-division; however, for service purposes, its area of jurisdiction may cover several sub-divisions by decree of the president of the Republic. According to section 13 sub (2), the court will be situated in the chief town of the sub-division but may hear matters outside its seat. Such hearings shall be referred to as 'circuit courts'. Section 14 of this law lays down the composition of the Court of First Instance; at the bench, there is a president, one or more magistrates, one registrar in chief and one or more registrars. At the preliminary inquiry, there are one or more examining magistrates, one or more registrars. At the legal department, a judicial officer hearing and determining all cases brought to the court. Section 15 of this law lays down the court's jurisdiction to hear civil, criminal, and labour matters, and also tries simple offences and related misdemeanours with damages of fine charged not more than 10,000,000 frs.

The Language Policy of Cameroon

The language policy and the legal system of Cameroon have something in common: the official languages, English and French. All legal documents are written in English and French, and courtroom discourses are conducted either in English or in French, depending on the legal district. However, apart from English and French, Cameroon has more than 250 national languages. Those national languages belong to three of the four language phyla existing in Africa (the Afro-Asiatic, Nilo-Saharan, and Niger-Kordofanian phyla). Rosendal (2008) argued that the appellation 'National Languages' reflects the idea of nationality alongside the idea of language-nation-state which was developed during the post era of the French revolution. Cameroon is not the only African nation referring to its languages as 'National Languages'. Many other ancient French colonies like Benin, Angola, and Mozambique also term their languages as such. While most African nations have incorporated their national languages in all public spheres, Cameroon relegated those languages to home usage. The implementation of a non-inclusive language policy in the legal setting brought in serious legal language-related problems.

As earlier mentioned, the Cameroon of today reflects the Cameroon of yesterday. During the colonial period, Britain administered just 20% of the Cameroon territory and the French 80%. Nowadays, French is spoken by

80% of the Cameroon population and English by 20% of the population. Even though the constitution stipulates that English and French are of equal status, in reality, this is not the case. The French language dominates both the formal and informal domains. All official documents are first published in French before been published in English and there are even some documents that are only published in French (for instance, *DECRET N° 93/035 DU 19 JANVIER 1993 Portant Statut Spécial des Personnels de l'Enseignement Supérieur*). The conflict that exists between English and French in Cameroon gives very little chance to the national languages which try as best as they can to find a place at the national level.

Rosendal (2008) stipulated that the major problem of Cameroon national languages is their number. Even if linguists generally approximate the number of national languages to 250, it is difficult to determine the exact number. There are too many national languages and it will be challenging to incorporate them all at the national level. And apart from national languages, linguists also registered new languages likes: Cameroon Pidgin English (CPE) and Camfranglais. CPE is mostly spoken in the two English-speaking Regions of Cameroon (the North-West and South-West Regions), and it is also timidly present in other French-speaking regions. Camfranglais is a youth language developed in the French-speaking regions. This youth language is a mixture of French, English, Pidgin English, and national languages like Ewondo, Bulu, and Duala. With all this panoply of languages, it becomes more and more necessary to review the language policy of Cameroon. However, the tendency towards the neglect of national languages gives rise to Language Endangerment. Many scholars denounced this rather alarming situation and some even went further to propose some language policy and planning. For example, Chiatoh and Akumbu (2014) advocated for the introduction of national languages in the educational sector.

Chiatoh and Akumbu (2014) argued that the implementation of an official bilingualism policy for more than 50 years (1961–2014) has significantly affected the quality of education in Cameroon. They recommended the introduction of national languages (mother tongues) in the educational system without eradicating the official languages. The debate on the introduction of mother tongues in the educational system is not only present in Cameroon but in Africa in general. In effect, many scholars and international organisations like UNESCO believe that the learning process is more spontaneous when teaching is being done in a language that learners understand the most (mother tongue). Thus, the use of mother tongues together with the two official languages can solve the language-related problems of the Cameroon educational system. Chiatoh and Akumbu's (2014) suggestion can also be applied in the legal setting. The present work suggests the introduction of mother tongues in the legal setting to ensure fluent discussions between legal professionals and lay-litigants during judicial proceedings.

The Legal Language-Related Problems

Language is central to all human activities. The human activity we are interested in here is the legal activity, specifically the language used during courtroom discourse. Scholars like Cotterill (2002), Coulthard and Johnson (2007, 2010), McMenamin (2010), Robert (2005), Shuy (2006), Solan (2002), and Tiersma (2002) attested of the scientific interest of language dynamics in legal settings. Two main factors can account for this: the legal jargon and the diversity of the stakeholders. The latter come from various backgrounds. On one side, we have legal professionals like judges, attorneys, lawyers, and so on, and on the other, we have lay-litigants like accused persons, plaintiffs, and witnesses. Both the stakeholders and the legal jargon bring in a striking language dynamic in courtrooms, especially in a country like Cameroon, a multilingual nation with more than 250 national languages and two exoglossic languages serving as official languages.

English and French are the languages through which law is enacted and this is at the expense of the more than 250 national languages of Cameroon. Yet, only 60% of the Cameroon population is literate in the two official languages. The remaining 40% are native speakers of Cameroon national languages solely, English and/or French being just second and/or third languages (Essono, 2001). The non-inclusive language policy of the legal system generated many language problems in courts, among which language barrier between legal professionals and lay-litigants. Indeed, judges, state counsels, and attorneys have been trained to exercise their function either in English or French.

Even though the law prescribes the presence of interpreters to assist lay-litigants who cannot communicate in English or French, those interpreters are rarely present in courtrooms because litigants cannot afford their services, and court authorities rarely provide their assistance. And when circumstances are such that the court authorities have no other choice than to provide an interpreter, the communication problems are still not solved. Indeed, community interpreters (as they are called) used during court proceedings in Cameroon are not trained. They are rather volunteers selected from the audience on the spot or from the street. Yet, it is recognised that the presence of untrained interpreters during court proceedings is more harmful than beneficial to the culprit (Hale, 2010). This book aims to analyse the illocutionary acts of both lay-litigants and legal professionals during courtroom discourse. The objective is to investigate how the use of exoglossic languages in a highly multilingual nation, with a scarcely literate population, constitutes a serious legal language-related problem.

Conclusion

The legal system and language policy of Cameroon are vestiges of the colonial past. Though in the 1960s those policies were presented as ultimate tools for the prosperity of Cameroon, nowadays, those colonial policies have become cloudy agents. The melting-up of foreign legal systems, customary laws, and exoglossic languages made the Cameroon legal system a hybrid system of law. National languages are excluded and foreign languages implemented, though 40% of the population are not literate in foreign languages. In other words, lay-litigants are judged in languages they do not master. Chapter 3 will determine how Forensic Linguistic Studies identified, analysed, and proposed solutions to legal language-related problems.

References

Anyangwe, C. (1987). *The Cameroonian judicial system*. CEPER.

Apprendre le droit. (2017, October 30). *What is the difference between common law and civil law?* Retrieved from http://www.apprendre-le-droit.fr/

Chiatoh, B. A., & Akumbu, W. P. (2014). Enhancing English language studies in Cameroon: The mother tongue perspective. *California Linguistic Notes, 39*(1), 23–47.

Cotterill, J. (2002). *Language in the legal process*. Palgrave Macmillan.

Coulthard, M., & Johnson, A. (2007). *An introduction to forensic linguistics: Language in evidence*. Routledge.

Coulthard, M., & Johnson, A. (2010). *The Routledge handbook of forensic linguistics*. Routledge.

Dame, H. G. (2015). *Common law reasoning and institution*. University of London.

Essono, J.-M. (2001). Le Cameroun et ses langues. In J.-M. Essono (Ed.), *Cameroun: Politique, langues, économie et santé* (pp. 61–87). L'Harmattan.
Fombad, M. C. (2015). Managing legal diversity: Cameroonian bijuralism at a critical crossroad. In V. P. Vernon, Y. M. Mohamed, & A. Koppel (Eds.), *Mixed legal systems, East and West* (pp. 101–119). Ashgate.
Gardinier, D. E. (1963). *Cameroon–United Nations challenge to French policy.* Oxford University Press.
Garner, B. A., & Black, H. C. (2009). *Black's law dictionary* (9th ed.). St. Paul, MN: West.
Hale, S. (2010). Court interpreting: The need to raise the bar—Court interpreters as specialized experts. In C. Malcolm & J. Alison (Eds.), *The Routledge handbook of forensic linguistics* (pp. 440–455). Routledge.
McMenamin, R. G. (2010). Forensic stylistics: Theory and practice of forensic stylistics. In C. Malcolm & J. Alison (Eds.), *The Routledge handbook of forensic linguistics* (pp. 487–508). Routledge.
Robert, A. L. (2005). Forensic linguistics: Applying the scientific principles of language analysis to issues of the law. *International Journal of the Humanities, 3*, 1–6.
Rosendal, T. (2008). *Multilingual Cameroon: Policy, practice, problems and solutions.* Gothenburg Africana Informal Series.
Rudin, H. R. (1938). *The Germans in the Cameroons 1884–1914: A case study in modern imperialism.* Yale University Press.
Shuy, W. R. (2006). *Linguistics in the courtroom: A practical guide.* Oxford University Press.
Solan, L. M. (2002). The Clinton scandal: Some legal lessons from linguistics. In J. Cotterill (Ed.), *Language in the legal process* (pp. 180–195). Macmillan.
Tiersma, M. P. (2002). The language and law of product warnings. In J. Cotterill (Ed.), *Language in the legal process* (pp. 54–72). Palgrave Macmillan.

CHAPTER 3

Forensic Linguistic Studies Outside the Borders of Cameroon

Introduction

Forensic Linguistics (FL) is a branch of Applied Linguistics that makes use of linguistic tools to solve the language problems of the legal and judicial setting. FL is defined as the study of language and the law, covering topics ranging from legal language and courtroom discourse to plagiarism. It also concerns the applied (forensic) linguist who is involved in providing evidence, as an expert, for the defence and prosecution in areas as diverse as blackmail, trademarks, and warning labels (Coulthard & Johnson, 2010). Thus, FL is delimited by the science of language and legal preferences such as those formulated by legal authorities (Groot, 2003). FL is a well-established field of study with an international organisation—*International Society of Forensic Linguistics,* an association—*The International Association for Forensic Phonetics* and an international journal—*The Journal of Speech, Language and Law.* To better analyse the language-related problems of Cameroon it will be worth noting the progress of Forensic Linguistic studies. In other words, the review of relevant Forensic Linguistics literature will provide me with extensive tools to describe and analyse Cameroon courtroom discourse. However, as demonstrated in Chap. 4, Forensic Linguistic studies are still poorly known in Cameroon in particular and Africa in general. Therefore, this chapter aims at outlining the evolution, the areas, the current debates, and the new directions of Forensic Linguistic studies.

E. M. K. Dissake, *Language and Legal Proceedings*,
https://doi.org/10.1007/978-3-030-76349-7_3

The Evolution of Forensic Linguistics

It is difficult to define the starting point of FL as a scientific discipline. However, the first practice of FL research was observed in 1968 in Britain by a linguist named Svartvic. In the early 1950s, a man called Timothy John Evans was convicted of the murder of his wife and child. After listening to the convict's confessions, the court declared him guilty and executed him in 1953. For many, Evans confessions were very troublesome. A journalist named Ludwig Kennedy even published the confessions in one of his articles. To eliminate doubts, Svartvic analysed the confessions using linguistic strategies. He quickly discovered that the two confessions had two different styles. Using linguistic evidence, he established that those confessions were not coming from the same person. Thus, Evans did not make those confessions and was certainly innocent. As a result of this linguistic study, the British judiciary system started fighting against the presentation of wrong confessions during proceedings and even put in place the presentation of three sorts of confessions: handwritten, audio recorded, and video recorded confessions (Farshad et al., 2016, p. 377).

FL was also introduced in the US as a result of unfair judicial treatment. Ernesto Miranda was arrested and accused of an armed robbery. During his arrest and interrogation, the officers never told Miranda his rights. Miranda started answering the officers' questions without the presence of a lawyer and without knowing that he was not compelled to do so. During the court of appeal, Miranda's lawyer condemned the actions of the officers and asked for the liberation of his client on the premise that the officers did not follow the legal procedure and did not respect the rights of his client.

Despite the evolution of FL, when compared with the 2400 years' history of Applied Linguistics, FL is a very young field of study (McMenamin, 2002, p. 84). In effect, before the twentieth century, FL was considered a branch of Applied Linguistics and not a field of study on its own. All literature related to FL was published under other disciplines like Discourse and Society, Gender and Language, General Applied Linguistics, Language and Culture, Discourse Analysis, Professional Policing Sciences, and Law (Linfoot, 2007, p. 07). The first journal dedicated to FL works was created in 1994 under the appellation *Journal of Forensic Linguistics* (now known as *The International Journal of Speech, Language and the Law*).

Even if FL is generally classified as a linguistic field of study, one does not need to be a well-renowned linguist to contribute to the advances of

FL. Many legal practitioners like, judges, lawyers, and police officers have excelled in the field. For instance, Alison Johnson, the co-author of the *Routledge Handbook of Forensic Linguistics*, was a police officer. Added to that, there are many psychologists, sociologists, translators, and interpreters who embarked themselves on FL studies. However, many forensic linguists like Coulthard and Johnson (2010), Farshad et al. (2016), Groot (2003), McMenamin (2002), Shuy (2006), Solan (2002), and Cotterill (2002b) stipulated that to be a good forensic linguist, you must be a good linguist, as no FL can be done without linguistics. As such, all those scholars who ventured into the field of FL in one way or the other initiated themselves to linguistic studies.

The Evolution of FL Beyond Europe and America

As discussed earlier, FL studies originated and developed in global North nations like Britain and America in the early 1950s. This is why the bulk of FL literature is written by American and European scholars. Nevertheless, in recent years, researchers from other geographic spheres embarked on the linguistics descriptions of distinct legal settings. For instance, Eades (2012) studied Australian judicial proceedings. She focused on cases involving Australian Aboriginal people who speak varieties of English. Eades (2012) used the linguistic theory of language ideology to measure the power imbalances between standard English and dialects of English in Australian courtrooms. The analysis reveals that legal professionals give little importance to evidence delivered in dialects of English. Language ideologies in Australian courtrooms contribute to the perpetuation of neocolonial control over Australian Aboriginal people.

Forensic discourse analysts accustomed scholars to the analysis of the discourse structures of judicial proceedings to highlight linguistic inequalities. Emphases are laid on the legal jargon of legal practitioners and the linguistic limitations of lay-litigants. Eades' (2012) analysis of Australian courtroom discourse goes beyond interactional practices; she studied instances and effects of language ideologies in courtroom discourse. Language ideologies are the beliefs and attitudes that shape speakers' relationships to their own and others' languages, mediating between the social practice of language and the socioeconomic and political structures within which it occurs. This concept prevailed in the study of minority languages and dialects, and how power relations can be revealed through everyday language use. In Australian courtrooms, Aboriginal witness often uses a variety of English which differ from the standard variety accepted in formal settings. During the cross-examination and the closing arguments of legal practitioners, the storytelling often differs from the witness's initial story. The legal practitioners endeavour to retell the story in the standard variety of English. This of course decontextualises the evidence. Eades (2012) argues that legal practitioners retell witness story in standard English for two main reasons: (1) it is the official variety of the nation, and (2) it is the variety used in Great Britain (the ancient colonial masters). In Australia, British English is known to be a noble, pure, dignified, strong, and true language. This language ideology has huge consequences on courtroom discourse and even beyond.

FL studies expanded on the Asian continent. The Chinese jurists Xin He and Yuqing Feng analysed the petitions discourse of Chinese courts. He and Feng (2016) studied the use of legal jargon during petition discourse between litigants (petitioners) and legal professional (petition officials). The research sheds light on the petitioners' legal consciousness and the operation of the petition system in China. He and Feng (2016) also determined why mismatched discourses occur in Chinese courts. They noted that petitioners fight to frame their disputes in legal terms, while the petition officials employed 'channeling discourse' to divert the petitioners to legal or extra-legal institutions. Hence, the discourses between the petitioners and the petition officials were mismatched. Litigants start calling their petitioning experiences injurious, blaming officials, and making new claims. Disputes are thus reproduced because of the language barrier.

FL studies spread in the African continent in very recent years. Much South African research shed light on the non-inclusive language policy of the legal system. Kaschula et al. (2020), Lubbe (2008), Hlophe (2000), Madumetsa (2010), and Ralarala et al. (2019) outlined some of the legal language problems of South Africa. For example, Ralarala et al. (2019) studied the themes and perspective in language and the law in Africa and beyond. Their research is an innovative contribution because it goes beyond the geographical spheres of Europe and America, it showcases original investigation on language and the law from Africa and beyond. The selected settings were rarely featured in FL research. As a matter of fact, till today, the field of FL is virtually unknown in Africa. But Ralarala et al. (2019) do not claim an absolute dormancy of FL research in Africa. For instance, they mentioned Moeketsi (1998, 1999a, 1999b) research on South Africa courtroom discourse. However, they regret that FL did not create more attraction and visibility in a continent where multilingual complexity and colonial legacy are norms. Ralarala et al. (2019) address four FL themes: (1) police investigative interviewing, (2) language practice in legal process, (3) language as evidence, and (4) forensic linguistic evidence. Those themes are developed under different geographical perspectives (Ghana, Mozambique, South Africa, Zimbabwe, Australia, the USA with respects to migrants from the Caribbean Islands).

The evolution of FL beyond Europe and America enriches the field. The Australian case study demonstrated that courtroom discourse analysis is not only limited to the structure of the discourse but also include concepts like languages ideologies. And in this book, I intend to highlight a different form of illocutionary acts used in Cameroon courtrooms. Indeed, complex multilingual nations that undergone colonialism often experience amazing linguistic realities. Yet, the literature review below, attest that the African setting has been neglected by FL researchers.

Areas of FL

The areas of FL evolve as the field develops. Nowadays, FL counts a number of areas: Auditory and Acoustic Phonetics, Forensic Semantics, Discourse analysis and pragmatics, stylistics and authorship identification, interpretation and translation, and so on. While some considered those areas as sub-branches of FL, others considered them as fields of their own. For example, stylistics in FL has been considered as a field on its own as observed in *The Cambridge Encyclopaedia of Language*. However, McMenamin (2002) argued that FL 'cannot be accurately understood when defined by synecdochic descriptions' (p. 86). The areas of FL that fall within the scope of this study (the analysis of Cameroon courtroom discourse) are: Discourse Analysis and pragmatics, and translation and interpretation.

The analysis of discourse is the study of language larger than a sentence (narratives and conversations), and the evaluation of speakers intended meaning in actual language use is the study of pragmatics (McMenamin, 2002). The main purpose of discourse and pragmatics in FL is to analyse spoken and written languages in legal contexts. Discourse in spoken and written languages is always embedded of variables like speakers, hearers, social levels, profession, literacy, topics, settings, and time. All these variables often lead to misinterpretation. This is why pragmatic analysis complements discourse analysis.

Courtroom discourse analysis is the study of court participants (legal professionals and litigants) speech acts. However, Chuanyou (2012), Hibbitts (1995), Jannedy and Mendoza-Denton (2006), Matoesian (2008), and Matoesian (2010) demonstrated that courtroom discourse involved more than speech acts, but it also involves pragmatics (contexts) and modalities (signs and gestures). Thus, to define the speech act of court participants, the context and the symbols of the speech should be specified. When uttering a word or a sentence, we also make use of signs like gaze, body movement, facial displays, head nods, and paralinguistic features to sustain the message we want to pass out. Gestures do not only facilitate the transfer of messages from a speaker to a hearer, but they also make speeches more natural.

In the domain of courtroom discourse analysis, modality studies give more evidence and demonstrate the sincerity of speakers. For instance, Chuanyou (2012) studied how American lawyers make use of body movements and facial expressions to defend their client. The modality of American lawyers is often beneficial to their clients because body gestures and facial expressions help to convince the jury. Yet, Cotterill (2002a), Coulthard (2002), and Shuy (2001a, b) courtroom discourse analysis focalised on the illocutionary acts of legal professionals and litigants. They aimed to demonstrate the power of language in the courtroom. Indeed, even if the embodiment of pragmatics and modalities in the analysis of discourse makes the study more elaborated, the language analysis alone makes the research coherent. Hence, my analysis is limited to the illocutionary acts of court participants.

It often happens that interpreters translate court participants' illocutionary acts. Translation is the replacement of textual material in one language by equivalent textual material in another language (Catford, 1995), and legal translation is the field of translation that transforms legal documents and material from one language to another, respecting the original meaning. Most often, legal documents like Penal Codes, Criminal Codes, and Constitutions need to be translated from one language to another so as to bring various types of international relations into practice for the sake of exchanging information and experience among law specialists of different countries. In Cameroon, for instance, all written texts are translated from English to French and vice versa. Cao (2010) argued that legal translation is a specialist or technical translation, a kind of translational activity that involves special language use, that is, language for a special purpose (LSP) in the context of law, or language for a legal purpose (LLP).

Legal translation is a specialise translation because it does not only require the translator to have sound language skills, he/she also needs to have excellent knowledge in law, various legislations, and international standards. For this reason, the translated text must be adequate from the legal point of view to attain a precise and professional result. This is particularly true in Cameroon, where legal translators do not only translate the language but also translate legal systems (from the Common to Civil laws and vice versa). However, legal translation can never be total or absolute. There are some concepts pertaining to a legal system that does not have equivalence in another legal system. For instance, Allard (2001) explained that in Canada (a bijural nation), legal translators do not always succeed to translate a legal document from one official language to another because each language (English and French) respects a legal system (the Common and Civil laws).

While translators replace textual material from one language to another, interpreters convey the meaning of the spoken word from a source language (SL) to a target language (TL). Interpretation is an exercise that becomes more complex in the legal setting. Interpreters used in courtrooms are called courtroom interpreters, and a more generic term is forensic interpreters. The term 'forensic interpreters' refers to all those who interpret in legal settings. Hale (2010) outlined three elements that complexify forensic interpretation: the legal terminology, the context, and the stake.

The first, the legal terminology, refers to terms that are specific to the legal profession. Those terms are used to convey legal doctrine in statutes, court decisions, and business contracts. Most legal institutions require forensic interpreters to be bilingual, that is, having a native-like control of at least two languages. However, a bilingual person does not necessarily have a rich repertoire of legal terms in both languages. Even monolinguals most often do not have a good mastery of the legal vocabulary of their first language (L1). Therefore, forensic interpreters just like legal translators need to have excellent knowledge of the law.

The second element, the legal context is one of the most complex settings as far as interpreting is concerned. In courtrooms, for instance, interpreters have to take into consideration the voices of adversary camps (the defence, the accusation, as well as the inquisitorial). Added to that, courtroom interpreters also have to consider tones, illocutionary and perlocutionary acts, as well as aspects of turn-taking to render their interpretation coherent.

The third element, the stake of the interpretation, call for the vigilance of the interpreters. After a trial, an accused person can either be convicted or released. Therefore, courtroom interpreters' roles in trials are essentials. Hale (2010) outlined key issues in courtroom interpretation. First, courtroom interpreters should not interpret words or sentences but should interpret discuss and apply pragmatics to assure the effective transfer of messages. Second, interpreters need aids and assistance. The participants can help the interpreter by being audible enough, and judges can make sure that before any session, interpreters are briefed with some background knowledge of the case so that they come prepared. Third, for very long trials, interpreters can work in pairs in order to take some breaks when tired. Hale's suggestions are rarely followed in Cameroon. Chapter 4 of this book describes Cameroon courtroom discourse and explains why forensic interpretation becomes very complex in Cameroon.

Current Debates in FL

During the last decays, linguists have extended FL debates. The debates are not more limited to courtroom discourse analysis, legal translation, and interpretation , but the debates now involve issues like question types, genres, multilingualism, and litigant's real linguistic abilities. However, it should be noted that the current debates in FL studies are not limited to the elements discussed below; indeed, the discussed elements are just in accordance with what is perceived in Cameroon.

One of the topics on which researchers' debates is the language of the law. Legal language (language of the law) is the language used by legal professionals in legal contexts; it is also being referred to as legal jargon. Legal language is divided into two: spoken and written legal language. The first, the spoken legal language refers to spoken discourse in legal settings like courtrooms and police stations. The form of spoken legal language frequently analysed is the formulations of the questions in courtrooms and police stations. Questions are the main components of courtroom discourse and police interviews. During trials and police interviews, lawyers and police officers formulate, reformulate, and repeat questions and reported speeches to obtain satisfactory answers (Holt & Johnson, 2010). In spoken legal language, linguists recently explore the socio-pragmatic uses of questions in police interviews and trials.

The second, the written legal language, refers to a written form of legal discourse. In written legal language, linguists explore the real-world problems that readers encounter when reading legal texts like Constitutions and Penal Codes. Linguists outlined the complexity of legal texts and suggest solutions to overcome the impairment of legal texts. For instance, Stygall (2010) suggested the involvement of language experts in the writing process of legal texts and the syntactic reduction of phrases or sentences to shortened paragraphs. In the context of Cameroon, it will not be enough to simplify the language of legal documents or the legal jargon of the court to solve legal language-related problems. As earlier mentioned, 40% of the Cameroon population are not-literate in the languages of the law (English and French) but are proficient in the national languages, thus, what is needed in Cameroon is an inclusive language policy.

A second topic of debate in FL is the courtroom genres. In the early periods of courtroom discourse, interactions were mainly between judges and defendants, but nowadays, lawyers dominate courtroom interactions, and this punched the advent of adversarialism in courtrooms. During trials, lawyers make use of open-speeches, narratives, examinations, cross-examinations, and close-speeches to defend their clients. In open-speeches, lawyers prepare the jury and present their client's inoffensive nature. During the examination and cross-examination, lawyers question their clients and witnesses. And during close-speeches, lawyers summarise what was said during the trial. Many linguistic elements in lawyers' speeches can be raised. For instance, in opening speeches, lawyers use strong verbs to capture and convince the jury of the inoffensive nature of their clients as demonstrated in the sentence below:

> *I can <u>assure</u> you that, this man seated here has always been a loving and caring husband and father.*

The lawyer made use of the verb 'assure' to persuade the jury. In the examinations and cross-examinations, lawyers use face-threatening strategies through methods like tone raising, repetitions, and reported speeches to intimidate a witness. And in the last phase of the trial, closing speech, lawyers' attitudes are more moderate, they try to gain the sympathy of the jury. Lawyers' oratory techniques are a rich domain of studies as far as FL is concerned. Chapter 5 will enrich the literature with a peculiar illocutionary act used by Cameroonian legal professionals.

Linguists also started debating on the effective participation of lay-litigants in judicial proceedings (lay participants in judicial process). Even though lawyers dominate the discussions in courtrooms, the participation of lay-litigants in trials cannot be neglected. Indeed, the field of FL was developed because of the language problems encountered by non-legal professionals (litigants). In courtrooms, lay participants are mostly children, second-language learners, youths, gang members, and intellectually impaired. The main characteristic of lay participants is their poor mastery of the court language and its rules. Ehrlich (2010) studied the speech acts of a rape victim whose poor language proficiency distorted her declarations:

L:	…And in fact just raising another issue that I would like you to help us with if you can, this business of you realizing when the line was getting blurred when you said "Look, I don't want to sleep with you," or words to that effect, yes, you remember that?
CD:	Yes!
L:	Well, when you said that, what did that mean or what did you want that to mean, not to have intercourse with him?
CD:	Yeah, I mean, ultimately, that's what it meant. It also, I mean –.
The Court:	You didn't want to sleep with him but why not, "Don't undue [sic] my bra" and "Why don't you knock it off"?
CD:	Actually, "I don't want"—"I don't want to sleep with you "is very cryptic, and certainly as he got his hands under my shirt, as he took off my shirt, as he undid my bra, as he opened my belt and my pants and pulled them down and I said, "Please don't, please stop. Don't do that. I don't want you to do that, please don't", that's pretty direct as well (Ehrlich, 2010, p. 271).

The victim's account of the rape was discredited by her wrong appreciation of the semantic and pragmatic meaning of the phrase, 'I don't want'. The victim even ended up admitting that the actual meaning of the phrase is very 'cryptic'. Inadequate language proficiency in court can have devastating effects. In Chap. 5, some legal professional recalls cases where litigants distorted their declarations because of their poor language competency.

A fourth topic of discussion in FL is the multilingual status of the legal settings. Human migration contributes to the linguistics heterogeneity of nations. No language is limited to a specific geographical location. It often happens that native speakers of French, English, and other languages are tried in Germany, Spain, Italy, and so on. Court stakeholder's linguistics diversity contributed to the analysis of diverse multilingual aspects like legal translation and interpretation and litigant's real language proficiency. Hale (2010) investigated the issues of interpretation in courts. In developed countries like the UK and the USA, courtroom interpreters assist non-native litigants. But, untrained interpreters most often worsen the situation of lay-litigants. There aren't just the speeches that need a translation, legal documents also. Many international organisations like the UN drafted many charters and laws applicable worldwide. For instance, the International Human Rights charter was translated into 370 languages. Forensic interpreters and translators are highly interested in the quality, reliability, and validity of such translations.

Naerssen (2012) discussed another aspect of multilingualism in courts, litigant's real language proficiency. Most often in the USA, non-natives involve in judicial matters claimed of having poor English language proficiency. But it was determined that some litigants hide their linguistics abilities to enjoy certain support. To remedy this, linguists developed strategies to detect the real language abilities of litigants, for instance, the Language Analysis and Determination of Origin (LADO), and the Alternating Language Story Retell Task. The first, LADO, is a method used by some governments to evaluate the claims of asylum seekers on their regional or national origins. The second, Alternating Language Story Retell Task, consists of telling the same story to a participant in his first language (L1) and second language (L2), but include some unique information in the L2. In case the participant succeeds in providing that unique information during his retelling of the story in his L1, he will then have proven that he has a good listening skill in his L2. With LADO and the Alternating Language Story Retell Task, many litigants who lied about their second-language proficiency were cut off. Yet, many litigants are having real language problems.

Researchers' Contributions to Forensic Linguistic Study

Following the earlier discussion, FL could be expected to be the study of courtroom language, which is only part of the field's scope. In fact, FL deals with a wide variety of instances of the interface between language, crime, and the law. These may include, among many other areas of research, courtroom discourse, interpretation and translation, legal language, police cautioning of suspects (for instance, the Miranda rights), authorship identification and attribution, the use of linguistic evidence and linguists as 'expert witnesses' in court, the treatment of vulnerable witnesses (children, rape victims, etc.), and police interviews. To highlight other major topics within Forensic Linguistics, a literature review of the works of some of its main contributors are introduced and reviewed.

- Roger W. Shuy

Roger W. Shuy is considered by many as a founding researcher of FL. His area of specialisation in FL is Discourse Analysis (DA), even though he is also interested in other areas like 'Pragmatics, Semantics, and Syntax' (Linfoot, 2007, p. 08), which in one way or the other are all related to DA. To demonstrate his contribution to FL, we will discuss two of his research works: Shuy (2001a, b, 2002a, b).

Shuy (2001a, b) research falls within the area of authorship identification and attribution. The study described and analysed a ransom note written in pencil and left at the door of the parents of a kidnapped child. The ransom note was written as such:

> Do you ever want to see your precious little girl again? Put $10,000 cash in a diaper bag. Put it in the green trash kan on
> the devil strip at corner 18th and Carlson.
> Don't bring anybody along.
> No kops!! Come alone! I'll be watching you.
> all the time. Anyone with you,
> deal is off and dautter is dead!!!

One of the first things that Shuy pointed out was the spelling errors, words like *kops*, *dautter*, and *kan*, were wrongly spelt. Moreover, Shuy wondered how someone can wrongly spell words like *daughter*, *can*, and *corps*, but successfully spell a word like *precious*. The first reason advanced was that the author of the note was trying to mask his identity by making conscious mistakes to appear uneducated. However, Shuy noted that the note contained much evidence stipulating that its author was literate and fluent in English. Not only did the author of the note correctly spell the word *precious*, but he also succeeded in spelling other words like *diaper* and *watching*. Added to that, the punctuation was appropriately done, words were correctly organised, and he was fluent in English.

Shuy finally concluded that the author of the note was an educated Akron. Educated because of the appropriate spelling of words, good knowledge of the English syntax, and a good mastery of punctuation marks. The expression 'devil strip' enabled Shuy to determine the geographical origins of the kidnaper. The expression is only used in Akron. Due to his observations, Shuy requested to know if the police had a native of Akron in their suspect list and they did. It was a 30 years old man, well-educated and a native of Akron. When interrogated, the man confessed his crime.

We can note two important points from Shuy's analysis. First, in the area of authorship identification and attribution forensic linguists define profiles, but do not identify individuals. This is why Shuy asked if in the list of suspects there was an educated Akron. Second, when individuals attempt to hide their identities by making conscious mistakes, there are cultural elements that cannot be hidden. Indeed, the author of the ransom note tried to hide his identity by making conscious spelling errors, but could not control his usage of tribal expressions like *devil strip*. Many are not conscious of the fact that, though they speak the same language with others, they do not speak that language in the same way. For instance, in Cameroon, francophones of the West region will say 'je vais sauf que partir' (I must leave), and francophone of the littoral region will say 'je dois absolument partir' (I absolutely must leave). Even if they speak the same language (Cameroon French), there are some distinctive features influenced by their mother tongues unconsciously present in their vocabulary. Furthermore, forensic linguists are field workers. Forensic linguists need to go to the field to collect raw data on language variations, distinctive features, and cultural influences. If Shuy was not a field worker, he would not have known that only Akron's say devil strip.

The second study, Shuy (2002a, b), falls within the area of expert witnesses. Shuy (2002a, b) argued that most often when an attorney asks for the help of a linguist, it is for three reasons: '(1) the attorney has never used a linguist before, (2) the case is so hopeless that desperation has already set in, or (3) the attorney has become aware of the importance of linguistic analysis for a case' (p. 03).

Several reasons can push a linguist to reject the request of an attorney. One reason is that the case goes against the beliefs and convictions of the linguist. An expert should never take a case personally neither should he take a side during his expertise. His only role is to analyse and present his conclusions to the court, even if the results are against the client of the attorney who requested assistance. Another reason should be that the linguist is aware of the fact that his/her testimony will be of no help to the attorney. Yet, this is difficult or even impossible to determine before the analysis of the data. Shuy thus proposes two steps to follow. In the first step, the expert should do a kind of rapid appraisal of the data, and in the second step, he/she should give a preliminary conclusion to the attorney who will decide on whether the analysis can help him in the defence of his client or not. Third, an expert is advised to reject the request of an attorney immediately after he realises that the attorney wants to direct his/her conclusions. There are some instances where attorneys ask questions like 'Is it your conclusion that my client is not guilty?' Experts never have to answer such questions. An expert neither wins nor loses a case. He just provides evidence gotten after the analysis of some data. An expert who goes as far as determining if a person is guilty or not discredits his analysis. Also, an attorney may be tempted to ask the expert a question like 'What did my client really mean here?' A linguist should never answer such a question because linguists and anyone else 'cannot get inside the minds of people' (Shuy, 2002a, b, p. 05). What a linguist can do is to detect patterns of language use.

However, Shuy worked as an expert witness in approximately 54 cases. Fortunately, the American judicial system accepts the expertise of linguists in various cases like trademarks and label disputes, defamation, language of contracts, and discourse analysis in criminal cases. Shuy admitted that cross-examinations in trials are highly emotionally drained. He compared the cross-examination to a doctoral oral examination. Thus, testifying in trials is not for the 'weak at heart'. The process does not only consume time but energy.

It happens frequently that linguists are called upon to assist attorneys whose clients are accused of horrible crimes, and in many instances, the linguist is regarded as corrupt or immoral being. It is thus necessary to state once more that, an expert linguist does not judge, but presents the conclusions of his analysis. As such, if during a cross-examination, an expert has to say things that can work against the client of the attorney who called for his assistance, he should promptly do so. Shuy even used the expression 'honour bound to answer truthfully about what I found' (Shuy, 2002a, b, p. 06). Many attorneys are aware of this fact; this is the reason why they mostly do not call experts in the bar, but they prefer to use the experts' analysis as a defence strategy. Thus, linguists are mostly used as consultants rather than as expert witnesses by attorneys.

In Africa in general and Cameroon in particular, linguists are not yet used as experts witness during judicial proceedings. Indeed, in the expert list of the judicial system of Cameroon, we find all types of experts such as doctors and economists, but linguists are still not included in the list. This may be due to ignorance of the field of Forensic Linguistics, its advances, and the use made of it in developed nations. Research work extending FL studies to the African continent (as this work attempts to do) will urge the introduction of the field in the legal settings of African states as is the case in Europe and the USA.

- Malcolm Coulthard

Malcolm Coulthard area of interest is discourse analysis, but he also developed an interest in the area of legal language. Coulthard (2002) demonstrated how the linguistic analyses of police verbal evidence can help in determining whose voice is present in a verbatim.

Before the advent of the Police and Criminal Evidence Act (PACE) in England, police officers had total control over the verbal evidence presented before the court. Yet, police officers never received any training on how to produce verbal evidence. Linguists often attested of the difficulty of producing verbatim evidence. However, the reliability and the validity of police verbal evidence were never disputed. It was even believed that police officers could listen to confessions and appropriately put them down in written form several hours after the interviews. This is why police verbal evidence was always presented in courts even when accused persons refuted them.

In their verbal evidence, police officers always portray themselves as serious gentlemen, doing all that is 'legally' possible to get confessions of accused persons during interviews. Coulthard (2002) present an extract of a police verbatim evidence:

DS:	Smith 'Right now Roy, DC Jones will read this over to you, then you can read it yourself. You can make any alterations you wish. Is that being fair with you?'
MORLEY:	replied 'Yes'.
DS:	Jones then read over to MORLEY the contemporaneous notes ... MORLEY read them and was invited to sign them.

MORLEY: then said 'No I can't … Nothing personal lads'.
DS: Jones said 'Look Roy, have we put anything down in these notes that you didn't say?'
MORLEY: replied 'No, I can't sign the notes, but at least you know the truth'.

In the extract above, police officers are painted as honest and fair person while the accused is painted as an inconsistent and untrustworthy being. Moreover, the use of nicknames like 'Roy', aimed at demonstrating the friendly atmosphere established by the officer. Whereas, sentences like '*No, I can't sign the notes, but at least you know the truth*' aimed at presenting the accused as a dishonest person. Much verbal evidence presented in court aimed at polishing the images of officers. Those verbal evidence are frequently disputed by the defence camps.

In 1985 after the presentation of ten handwritten verbal evidence typed by the police, Ashley King was accused and convicted for the death of an old lady. Coulthard (2002) presented an extract of verbal evidence:

Q: When we saw you last Saturday you told us that you didn't go out at all on the evening of Monday the 4th of November. Are you still saying that's true?

A: Yes, I'm sure that's right.

Q: It can be difficult thinking back Ash, so think very carefully, it's very important.

A: Aye, I'm sure about that. I never left the house.

Q: We've interviewed some people who say you were out that night? [sic].

A: I don't think so.

Q: Think very carefully about it, it's important.

A: I think that was the night we got the tyres, is that what you mean?

Q: Tell us about it.

A: Billy, Berti and Melley called for us and we went up the bank and got some tyres.

Q: What time was this?

A: They came for us about six o'clock.

Q: Who's Berti?

A: I don't know his second name but he's from Shiney.

Q: When you say you got some tyres, do you mean you stole them?

A: Aye, I think so.

I then cautioned KING.

Q: Where did you get the tyres from?

A: It's a place next to the garage, it's near the pit.
Q: Do you know the name of the premises?
A: Tyre Services I think, but I'm not sure.

Once more, the police officer is presented as a patient man while the accused (King) is presented as a non-reliable person. First, King admitted his crime only after several hours of interviews. Second, the officer never urged the accused to say the truth nor did he mount pressure on him. He remained very patient and never contradicted the accused. Thus, when the defence rejected this evidence on the pretext that the police mounted pressure on their client, the court never took note of this rejection and the accused was convicted. During the court of appeal, Coulthard demonstrated that the verbal evidence presented during the first trial did not correspond to what the accused said, but were rather persuasive dramatised literary texts orchestrated by police officers and written several hours after the interview.

Coulthard (2002) also analysed the police verbal evidence of the murder case of a teenage boy. In 1978 four men were arrested for the murder of a teenage boy in Birmingham. One of those men, Patrick Molloy, confessed the crime and incriminated the three others. Later on, Patrick Molloy withdrew his confession on the claim that he was misled by the officer who presented fake confession supposedly coming from one of the three boys. The police refuted all those allegations, and the other confession was never presented during the first trial. As such, Patrick Molloy and his three accomplices were convicted.

During the first trial, Molloy insisted on the fact that the verbal evidence was created by officers and dictated to him. In other words, Molloy claimed that the real authors of the confession were the officers and not him. Molloy and his three accomplices were convicted because of the total similarity of Molloy's confession and Molloy's police interview. The jury gave their verdict based on the fact that both the confession and the interview were Molloy's words. Yet, in linguistics, it is argued that someone cannot say a story in different contexts, using similar words and expressions. The ESDA test done on the original handwritten version of Molloy's confession, before the hearing of the appeal, attested that the confession was not written by Molloy. Therefore, Molloy and his accomplices were declared innocent. But, Molloy had long died in prison and it is only his three accomplices who were released.

The third court case analysed in Coulthard (2002) was that of Derek Bentley and Chris Craig. In 1952 two teenagers Derek Bentley and Chris Craig aged 19 and 16, respectively, were arrested for the murder of a police officer. It was Chris Craig who shot at the officer. Though Craig killed the officer, Bentley was jointly charged with murder. At the end of the trial, Craig was sentenced to life imprisonment, because he was legally a minor, and Bentley was sentenced to death. Bentley's family fought against this verdict for 46 years and they succeeded to change the verdict through linguistic evidence. During Bentley's original trial, his attorney pleaded with the jury to be sure of two things: '(i) that Bentley knew Craig had a gun, and (ii) that he instigated or incited Craig to use it' (Coulthard, 2002, p. 28).

The evidence presented by the prosecution to satisfy these two points was essentially linguistics. For the first point, the prosecution stipulated that Bentley knew that Craig had a gun because during his confession Bentley said 'I did not know he was going to use the gun'. Bentley said 'the gun' and not 'a gun' because he knew that Craig had a gun. Second, in the verbal evidence it was stated that during Bentley and Craig's confrontation with the four police officers, Bentley shouted to Craig 'Let him have it, Chris'. Thus, Bentley incited Craig to shoot. All these evidence presented by the prosecutor were taken from officers' verbal evidence, and officers were trusted by the jury and even the judge.

During the Court of Appeal, Coulthard demonstrated that someone can say the gun instead of 'a gun' simply because, throughout the conversation, the gun was mentioned. Thus, 'the gun' refers to what was said before. As such, during the police interview, officers had certainly made mention of the gun throughout the conversation, and this was certainly the reason why Bentley said 'the gun' and not 'a gun'. This first point deconstructed the prosecution allegation of Bentley knowing that Craig had a gun and at the same time discredited the officers. Indeed, officers ignored that they were the first to make mention of a gun during their interview and that Bentley's answer was in relation to their question. This untrustworthy situation allowed the jury to question the fact that Bentley really said 'Let him have it, Chris'. Actually, one of the three officers denied that Bentley uttered that sentence. 'In August 1998, 46 years after the event, the Lord Chief Justice criticised his predecessor's summing-up and allowed the Appeal against conviction' (Coulthard, 2002, p. 33).

Examples like what was stated above confirm that verbatim evidence cannot be left in the hands and control of officers, and the introduction of

PACE was one of the major advances of the British judicial system. Moreover, linguistics expertise may be of paramount importance in some cases. Yet, linguistics evidence is rarely used in the global South. Nevertheless, the legal cases presented in Chap. 3 attest that Cameroon needs the expertise of linguists in various judicial cases.

- Janet Cotterill

Janet Cotterill main domains of interest in FL are, interviewing vulnerable witnesses such as children, handicapped persons, and those relying on interpreters; effective lawyer-client communication strategies; interpretation and communication of legal rights; and courtroom discourse in general. Cotterill (2002a) presented the aspect of intertextuality in trials using the criminal and civil trials of O. J. Simpson. Cotterill (2002a) research defined and analysed two main aspects of courtroom discourse: Narratives and Intertextuality.

First, narratives. In the judicial context, narratives are 'essentially multi-perspectival and multi-voiced. By the time a case reaches the courtroom, it has potentially been subject to a large number of retellings in a variety of contexts, including police interviews, grand jury and plea-bargaining sessions as well as pre-trial indictment and arraignment hearings' (Cotterill, 2002a). Actually, during trials, witnesses are forced to tell and retell their stories. At the end of the trial, witness accounts are not more the same. Perhaps, forensic narratives most often contain conflicting ideas and this result from the fact that prosecutors and defence barristers during the phases of the examination introduce different perspectives of events and/or stories. Thus, a witness can repeat a story using a different and/or conflicting storyline.

For the credibility of a witness, he/she has to be capable to repeat the same story without any conflicting ideas. However, this is very difficult to achieve as the storyline of the witness is highly influenced by the examination of barristers. As such, Cotterill identified three types of narratives: *spontaneous, prompted, and elicited narratives.* Each of these types is in different degrees influenced by barristers. Barristers are always fighting to present events that promote.

Second, intertextuality. Intertextuality in forensically oriented narratives 'concerns the extent to which any single text incorporates and/or acknowledges its interaction with other texts, both past and future, paradigmatic and syntagmatic' (Cotterill, 2002a, b, p. 150). The two phases, the criminal and the civil trials, of O. J. Simpson, illustrate the concept of intertextuality in courtroom discourse. O. J. Simpson was accused of the murder of his wife and her lover. Robert Heidstra was the main witness of both trials. In the criminal trial, Robert Heidstra was called by the defence under subpoena, but in the civil trial, he voluntarily took the side of the prosecution. Heidstra was the only eyewitness; thus, the exact time of the murder and the colour of the weapon (a car) could be confirmed only by him. Cotterill (2002a, b) used Heidstra's testimonies during both trials to exemplify intertextuality in courtroom discourse.

Extract 1 (Criminal Trial)

1 Q: (BY MR PETROCELLI) Did the car that you saw that evening look 2 like the one in the photo?
3 A: It was—it resembled a car like this, yes. For sure, *I couldn't say exactly*
4 this car, but it resembled the size of the car.
5 Q: And the color?
6 A: *White.*

Extract 2 (Civil Trial)

1'Q: (BY MR BAKER) Now, one other thing: You testified, did you not, that the 2 color was light or white?
3'A: No. It was definitely white, sir.
[...]
15 'Q: What color was the color?'
16 'A: *Very light color, white or light.*'
17 'Q: White or light?'
18 'A: *It was white or something.*'
19 Q: (MR BAKER TO HEIDSTRA) Does that refresh your recollection, sir?
20 A: It was white, definitely white.
21 Q: So it wasn't white or light?
22 A: No, it was white.
23 Q It wasn't white or light?
24 A: It was white.
25 Q: Thank you.
26 (MR BAKER) Nothing further.

In lines 1 and 2 of extract 2, the defence barrister made use of Heidstra's criminal trial narratives to ask questions related to the colour of the car. The main aim of this intertextuality was to discredit Heidstra, to present him as an unreliable witness, who could say one thing during a trial and say something else in another trial. In lines 16 and 18 of extract 2, Heidstra could no more determine the exact colour of the car, meanwhile in extract 1, he suggested white colour. However, narratives and intertextuality can be outlined in courtroom discourse analysis when participants have good control of the court language. In courtroom discourse involving lay participants, as is the case in Cameroon, we can rarely analyse the narratives and intertextuality.

- Peter M. Tiersma

Tiersma mainly worked on four areas of FL: jury instruction, contract law, legal language, and implicature in perjury. Tiersma (2002) argues that warnings on product labels are rarely understood by the consumer and this impairment often caused injuries to consumers. Thus, warnings on product labels are an essential means through which damage can be reduced. This domain of language and the law, that is 'Product liability/ Product Warnings' is a relatively recent development in FL. In many developed countries like America, product manufacturers have been held responsible for the damages caused by their products on users. It has been acknowledged that the labels of many products do not contain adequate warnings. In effect, even if a product serves useful functions and is designed and manufactured carefully, risks and damages are never excluded. Perhaps adequate warnings should be present in every product. Tiersmas (2002) aim was to demonstrate that products warnings are not particularly effective.

'Adequacy' of product warning is a legal standard in America, a court explained this standard as such: 'focus on the language used and the impression that the language is calculated to make upon the mind of the average user of the product' (Tiersma, 2002, p. 55). In other words, product warnings must be calculated to come to the attention of the user and the content of the warning should be understandable to the user. Now comes the question of '*who is the user?*' and '*what is his/her level of comprehension?*' The American law requires that warnings should be understandable to the 'ordinarily intelligent person' or the 'average person', but also recognise that some product warnings like drugs are more difficult to render comprehensible for ordinary or average persons. As such, the interpretation of the warning is left to the responsibility of the physician prescribing the drug. Thus, physicians are here considered as *'learned intermediaries'*. However, they do not always play this role. Most often, the interpretation of the warning of the drug is left in the hands of patients.

Warnings should not only have as the target population, ordinary or average persons but should also include in their target, 'below average persons'. Tiersma (2002) suggested that 'the standard should be that a warning should be understandable to a substantial majority of users' (p. 56). He illustrates this necessity with the warning present in rubbing alcohol, readily available in American drug stores:

FOR EXTERNAL USE ONLY

- *Will produce serious gastric disturbances if taken internally.*
- *In case of accidental ingestion, seek professional assistance or contact a Poison Control Center immediately*

Tiersma (2002) argued that an alcohol addict or even an average person will hardly understand the expression 'for external use only' on a product on which is written ALCOHOL. For an average person, 'external use only' will mean that she/he have to drink the alcohol outdoors and/ or in the open air. The warning continues with the concept of 'gastric disturbances' which is a concept rarely understood even by ordinary or average persons. We also have the word 'ingestion', which is also problematic. Indeed, concepts like external use only, gastric disturbances, and ingestion are highly formal and obscure terminologies. Same goes with other terms like Indication and Contraindication, both terms are frequently seen in warning labels, but are mostly used by medical providers.

Tiersma (2002) also noted the use of auxiliaries on product warning labels. Auxiliaries are commonly defined as weak verbs; thus, the presence of an auxiliary in a warning renders it weak. This is how auxiliaries are often used in warnings:

- *It <u>may</u> damage the kidneys*
- *Smoking <u>may</u> be hazardous to your health*

Many users will think that the presence *may* simply mean that the chances of coming across such injuries are very low. As such, they are not concerned with the warning. Meanwhile, in the case of cigarettes, for instance, it is unfair to say that the smoking of cigarettes *may* be hazardous to health. One can even consider this to be a lie. Hence, warnings should not be written in a weak or indirect form, as this may push the user to undermine the risk of the product.

Furthermore, Tiersma (2002) explain that warnings should neither say too little nor too much. When a product points out too many dangers, less serious ones may overshadow more serious ones. However, when a warning says too little the users may underestimate the risks and the dangers of the product. Also, the font size of warnings is most often too small and this can cause users not to lay eyes on them. As rightly pointed out by Tiersma, 'Important or urgent messages are spoken loudly or shouted for emphasis in speech. In a written text, large/capital letters carry out that function' (p. 58).

As far as the adequacy of product warnings is concerned, American courts showed concern on issues like font size, the location of the warning, the problem of mixed messages, overly weak warnings, and information overload. But, less interest has been given to the notion of bilingualism or multilingualism. In effect, it will be naïve to think that a product manufactured in the US will only be used by English native speakers. Because of goods exportation, a product produced in America can be used in France, Cameroon, Spain, and so on. And even if the product is only used in America, America is inhabited by people of different linguistic background. A product warning should always have an aspect of multilingualism. However, it is very difficult to transmit a message in different languages considering that, it is not only the language that matters but also the culture. To overcome the problem of multilingualism in product warnings, Tiersma (2002) proposed the use of symbols, pictograms, and colours. But pictograms and colours are culturally determined. However, the most important is to transmit relevant information to a higher number of people, and this cannot be achieved only through languages but also through the use of attractive figures like symbols, pictograms, and colours.

Another way of ensuring adequate warning in product labels is the use of imperative and informative constructions. Thus, instead of saying *for external use*, a manufacturer may say '*don't swallow this product!*' and can even go as far as combining an imperative construction to an informative one: *do not drink—this product is harmful if swallowed*. Warning languages should always be ordinary with the use of concrete nouns, action verbs, strong auxiliary verbs, symbols, and so on. Indeed, instead of saying 'for external use', gastric disturbances, and accidental ingestion, it will be preferable to say: *'do not drink'*, *'you will get severe stomach problems'*, *'if you drink this product'*.

The reason why most manufacturers do not yet respect the principle of adequate warning is that they are not subjected to intense governmental and legal regulations. However, many manufacturers have worked on the adequacy of their product warnings, but they still endeavour to embellish the risk and damages of their products because they fear that if the risks are directly presented, customers may run away from the product. This is why product warnings, will always need to be scrutinised by an independent body. Even if this book does not talk about warning of product labels, it is still important to talk about the points developed in Tiersma (2002) so as to show how FL studies evolved over time. FL studies are not more limited to courtrooms, police stations, or prisons, but now touches industries and their products.

- Lawrence M. Solan

Lawrence M. Solan domains of interest are legal interpretation, the attribution of responsibility and blame, and the role of the expert in the courts. Solan (2002) studied the Clinton trial scandal, the former American president accused of sexual harassment. Throughout Clinton judicial proceeding, the emphasis was placed on the difference between two concepts: lie and deception.[1] The prosecution aimed at proving that both lies and deceptions are acts of perjury. However, Solan (2002) argued that a 'lie' is a lie, and a 'deception' is a deception, and what is considered as an act of perjury is a 'lie' and nothing else.

As of 1994, President Clinton was under various sorts of congress investigations, and one of the most serious was his alleged roles in a real-estate venture in Arkansas, called White-water. This case was later on merged with Paula Jones' accusation of sexual harassment. It was under this atmosphere that the news of Clinton's relationship with Monica Lewinsky arose. As Kenneth Starr, the appointed head of investigation, had less evidence against Clinton on Jones' case, he decided to emphasise on Clinton's relationship with Lewinsky to demonstrate that Clinton was a womaniser. Clinton was not prepared for an examination on his

[1] Speech acts whose effect is to leave the listener with the impression that something is true that the speaker knows to be false Solan (2002).

relationship with Lewinsky, this is why Clinton's answers throughout the examination were never clear. Starr then empanelled a grand jury to investigate on whether Clinton was dishonest at the Jones deposition.

During the deposition stage, Clinton's lawyer argued that his client never had sex with Lewinsky, and Starr questioned Clinton on the veracity of the lawyer's allegations.

Q: Your—that statement is a completely false statement. Whether or not Mr. Bennett knew of your relationship with Ms. Lewinsky, the statement that there was no sex of any kind in any manner, shape, or form with President Clinton was an utterly false statement. *Is that correct?*

Clinton: *It depends upon what the meaning of the word 'is' is.* If 'is' means is, and never has been, that's one thing. If it means, none was a completely true statement. (Grand Jury Transcript, pp. 509–10)

Clinton's vague answer gave room to a series of questions concerning his supposed sexual relation with Lewinsky. Because Clinton delimits his definition of sexual intercourse to oral sex, he denied having sex with Lewinsky. Indeed, Clinton was not asked if he had oral sex with Lewinsky, but rather if he had sexual intercourse with her. Hence, the question was whether Clinton lied and therefore committed an act of perjury. However, the United States federal jury definition of perjury[2] never included deceptions.

Nothing in the perjury definition prevents witnesses from making use of deception. Nonetheless, if we take into consideration Austin's (1962) perlocutionary effect, a speaker utterance should always be in accordance with the hearer's state of mind. Anyhow, to establish that an answer to a question is a lie, we should verify if the listener understood the meaning of the question within the context. To illustrate this, Solan took the case of someone needing a dollar to put in a soda machine. He may ask, 'who has a dollar?' If someone having 12 dollars says 'I have a dollar', would we consider his answer to be a lie? No, because he understood the question

[2] (1) having taken an oath ... that he will testify, declare, depose, or certify truly, or that any written testimony, declaration, deposition, or certificate by him subscribed, is true, willfully and contrary to such oath states or subscribes any material matter which he does not believe to be true... (Solan, 2002, pp. 183–4)

within a given context. Though he will leave the listener with the wrong impression of him having just a dollar, we cannot say that he lied. Solan added that 'literal falsity is a standard imposed after we decide which possible meaning of a question the witness understood' (Solan, 2002, p. 186).

The analysis of Solan (2002) research is relevant to the present work because in Cameroon, lay-litigants facing difficulties with the court language usually expressed themselves in a disjointed manner, and this is often considered as an act of perjury. Litigants' response may seem untruthful simply because they did not understand the meaning of the question within the context. The court extracts provided in Chap. 3 will demonstrate that some lay-litigants' answers are not adequate because they do not have an appropriate definition of terms.

- Gerald R. McMenamin

Gerald R. McMenamin domain of interest is forensic stylistics and he also works as an expert witness. McMenamin (2010) defined the concept of forensic stylistics in detail. He included in his description concepts like language, dialects, idiolects, linguistic variations, style, and stylistics. In fact, forensic stylistics is the combination of the above listed areas and/or branches of linguistics.

Language is defined as a system of communication used by people of a given nation, community, society, and so on. A dialect is a variety of a language. An idiolect is a variety of language developed by the individual speaker. And linguistic variation, the focal point of stylistic analysis, helps in identifying dialects and idiolects. Labov was one of the first researchers to identify factors that promote linguistic variation. Such factors are mostly external. For instance, we have factors like age, sex, social class, and region of origin.

On the one hand, we have the concept of style in the overall study of stylistics. We can easily assimilate style to fashion. In effect, we all have our particular ways of dressing, styling our hairs, and using cosmetics. It is all those peculiarities that constitute who we are, and which distinguishes us from others. Style and/or linguistic style follow the same principle. We all live in linguistic communities, but we always succeed in one way or the other, consciously or subconsciously, to develop our own linguistic style. Thus, linguistic style is 'the result of what an individual selects to use from the array of linguistic tools available to his or her own group or other groups of speakers' (McMenamin, 2010, p. 488). In addition to that, linguistic style is acquired and developed right from childhood, and once completely acquired it becomes very stable/frequent/recurrent in us.

On the other hand, we have stylistics in linguistics. Linguistic stylistics is defined as 'the scientific interpretation of style-markers as observed, described and analysed in the language of groups and individuals' (McMenamin, 2010, p. 488). The most important aspect of linguistic stylistics is style-markers. Style-markers are the 'observable results of the habitual and usually unconscious choices an author makes in the process of writing' (McMenamin, 2010, p. 488). There are two types of style-markers: Choice of optional forms and deviation from a norm. The second, deviation from a norm, mainly comes as a result of a low level of education. Linguistic stylistic analysis is a time and energy consuming exercise, which involves many scientific models and processes put forward by many renowned researchers.

McMenamin (2010) made use of Wachal's (1966) three models of stylistic analysis: ***resemblance***, ***consistency***, and ***population***. The resemblance model is the first step in linguistic stylistics, and it is used when external factors are so narrowed that they can lead to the identification of the unknown author. We can take, for instance, the case of a questioned blackmail letter, where the author gave so many details on the private life of the victim, details that are only known to one person. This person can then be identified as the author of the blackmail letter. As for the consistency model, it is used to determine if the same author used various written styles. The population model is used when the pool of potential authors is large (McMenamin, 2010, p. 490).

Wachal's (1966) models made use of terms like *questioned* and *unknown*. In forensic stylistic science, those terms are basics. A researcher only engages in a forensic stylistic analysis when he has a questioned text written by an unknown author. Throughout his analysis, the researcher will make use of quantitative and qualitative analysis. The qualitative analysis consists of a description of style gotten after a systematic observation. Whereas, quantitative analysis consists of various measurement styles like 'frequency distributions, standard error of difference, t-Test, analysis of variance, proportion test, chi-square, coefficient of correlation, and probability of occurrence calculations' (McMenamin, 2010, p. 491).

Although Forensic stylistics received various praises from linguists as well as legal practitioners, McMenamin (2010) acknowledge the fact that forensic stylistics has various limitations among which its arbitrary and subjective nature. The criteria for selecting style-markers are always full of preconceived stereotypes and prejudices. Another limitation is the concept of frequency of occurrence of a stylistic variable. No one has ever succeeded to establish an appropriate frequency of occurrence before getting into a valid and reliable result. One of the most significant limitations of forensic stylistics is the determination of the level of conscious intervention in the choice of words by an author. How well are we sure that the variables observed are not conscious choices of words and/or style? Linguists should also never neglect the fact that many legal systems do not welcome the use of forensic stylistic analysis. In Cameroon for instance, this method of analysis has never been exploited during forensic investigations. One reason may be that FL is still an unknown field of study in Cameroon.

New Directions of FL

In pointing out some new debates and directions of FL, Coulthard and Johnson (2010) did not pretend to predict the future, but they only attempted to look forward to some of the upcoming advances of FL.

They started by looking forward at how forensic discourse analysis will no longer rely on the words and utterances of speakers but will also take into consideration body gestures to capture the complete sense and meaning of utterances. Thus, forensic discourse analysis considers multimodality aspects. However, this domain which is now studied by some linguists encounters one major challenge: access to videotapes of police interviews and courtroom trials. Even though many developed nations have worked on the introduction of cameras in courtrooms and police stations, in many instances, videotapes are nowhere to be found, and even when they can be found, linguists are rarely given access to such evidence.

With the spread of terrorism all over the world, FL can bring some expertise in terrorist cases. In many instances, the law is caught by human rights when interviewing or judging terrorist suspects. It thus becomes difficult to fight against terrorism while respecting human rights. Linguists can thus work towards reassessing and prioritising the suspect's rights.

Moreover, computation is a domain that has never received adequate attention in FL. Looking at how the world completely depends on computation nowadays; it will be judicial to make use of the power of computation in linguistic analyses. It is true that in the domain of forensic phonetics, phoneticians make use of computer programs in their voice analysis, but computers can be used for other purposes. For instance, linguists can make use of computers in the creation and analysis of large-scale corpora, this will enable forensic analyses to be quantitatively accountable and measurable.

It was also noted that many legal professionals do not understand and do not accept the role of FL in law. For many, FL is a redundant field of study. This is why the analyses of some expert's witness are not taken as seriously as ADN analysis. Coulthard and Johnson (2010) suggested a greater cross-disciplinary discussion and exchange of ideas since lawyers and judges are woefully unaware of the existence of FL benefits.

Conclusion

The field of FL was enriched by the creation of journals, associations, meetings, and various FL research. FL got developed to such an extent that its branches and sub-branches (i.e. Auditory Phonetics, Acoustic Phonetics, Semantics, Courtroom Discourse Analysis, stylistics and authorship identification, legal translation and interpretation, etc.) are now considered as fields on their own. Scholars like Shuy, Coulthard, Solan, Tiersma, and Cotterill have developed and open debates in FL. Yet, Coulthard and Johnson (2010) noted other domains of FL which still need to be developed. Although Forensic Linguistics has become a well-established field of study, it is still absent in several African nations. FL research focuses on the legal language problems of developed nations, the African setting is still very absent from the literature. For instance, Coulthard and Johnson (2010), Drew (1992), and Matoesian (2008) analysed the courtroom discourse of England; Shuy (2001a, b, 2002a, b, 2006), and Cotterill (2002a, b) studied the legal language-related problems of the American courtrooms; Groot (2003) describe the aspect of language and law of the Netherland courtrooms; Eades (2012) studied the case of Australia. And He and Feng (2016) analysed the discourse of Chinese courtrooms. The literature review allows me to argue that the analysis of Cameroon courtroom discourse, in Chap. 4 , brings in a new dynamic to the overall domain of discourse analysis in Forensic Linguistic studies.

References

Allard, F. (2001). *The Supreme Court of Canada and its impact on the expression of bijuralism*. Supreme Court of Canada.

Austin, J. L. (1962). *How to do things with words*. Oxford University Press.

Cao, D. (2010). Legal translation: Translating legal language. In C. Malcolm & J. Alison (Eds.), *The Routledge handbook of forensic linguistics* (pp. 78–94). Routledge.

Catford, J. (1995). *A linguistic theory of translation*. Oxford University Press.

Chuanyou, Y. (2012). Appreciate others' beauty as well as one's own: A contrastive multimodal discourse analysis of two courtroom trials. In S. Tomblin, N. MacLeod, R. Sousa-Silva, & M. Coulthard (Eds.), *Proceedings of the international association of forensic linguists' tenth biennial conference* (pp. 73–91). Centre for Forensic Linguistics.

Cotterill, J. (2002a). 'Just one more time…': Aspects of intertextuality in the trials of O. J. Simpson. In J. Cotterill (Ed.), *Language in the legal process* (pp. 147–161). Palgrave Macmillan.

Cotterill, J. (2002b). *Language in the legal process*. Palgrave Macmillan.

Coulthard, M. (2002). Whose voice is this? Invented and concealed dialogue in written records of verbal evidence produced by the police. In J. Cotterill (Ed.), *Legal language in the process* (pp. 19–33). Palgrave Macmillan.

Coulthard, M., & Johnson, A. (2010). *The Routledge handbook of forensic linguistics*. Routledge.

Drew, P. (1992). Contested evidence in courtroom cross-examination: The case of a trial for rape. In P. Drew & J. Heritage (Eds.), *Talk at work* (pp. 470–520). Cambridge University Press.

Eades, D. (2012). The social consequences of language ideologies in courtroom cross-examination. *Language in Society, 41*(4), 471–497.

Ehrlich, S. (2010). Rape victims: The discourse of rape trials. In C. Malcolm & J. Alison (Eds.), *The Routledge handbook of forensic linguistics* (pp. 265–280). Routledge.

Farshad, R., Sani, K. A., & Moghadam, K. (2016). Forensic linguistics in the light of crime investigation. *Pertanika Journals of Social Sciences & Humanities, 24*(1), 375–384. Retrieved from http://www.pertanika.upm.edu.my/

Groot, G. R. (2003). *Language and law*. Maastricht University Press.

Hale, S. (2010). Court interpreting: The need to raise the bar—Court interpreters as specialized experts. In C. Malcolm & J. Alison (Eds.), *The Routledge handbook of forensic linguistics* (pp. 440–455). Routledge.

He, X., & Feng, Y. (2016). Mismatched discourses in the petition of Chinese courts. *Law & Social Inquiry, 41*(1), 212–241.

Hibbitts, B. J. (1995). Making motions: The embodiment of law in gesture. *Journal of Contemporary Legal Issues, 51*, 51–82.

Hlophe, J. M. (2000). Official languages and the courts. *South African Law Journal, 117*(4), 690–696.

Holt, E., & Johnson, A. (2010). Legal talk: Socio-pragmatic aspects of legal talk—Police interviews and trial discourse. In M. Coulthard & A. Johnson (Eds.), *The Routledge handbook of forensic linguistics* (pp. 21–37). Routledge.

Jannedy, S., & Mendoza-Denton, N. (2006). Structuring information through gesture and intonation. *Interdisciplinary Studies on Information Structure, 3*, 199–244.

Kaschula, H. R., Docrat, Z., & de Vries, A. (2020, April 16). *Why using just one language in South Africa's courts is a problem*. Retrieved from The Conversation: https://theconversation.com/why-using-just-one-language-in-south-africas-courts-is-a-problem-134911

Linfoot, K. (2007). *Forensic linguistics, first-contact police interviews, and basic officer training* (PhD dissertation). University of Florida, Florida.

Lubbe, H. J. (2008). *The right to language in court: A language right or a communication right?* University of the Free State.

Madumetsa, K. C. (2010). *Law and language: Solution for multilingual societies*. University of Venda.

Matoesian, G. M. (2008). You might win the battle but lose the war: Multimodal, interactive, and extralinguistic aspects of witness resistance. *Journal of English Linguistics, 36*(3), 195–218.

Matoesian, G. (2010). Multimodality and forensic linguistics: Multimodal aspects of victim's narrative in direct examination. In M. Coulthard & A. Johnson (Eds.), *The Routledge handbook of forensic linguistics* (pp. 541–557). Routledge.

McMenamin, R. G. (2002). *Forensic linguistics: Advances in forensic stylistics*. CRC Press.

McMenamin, R. G. (2010). Forensic stylistics: Theory and practice of forensic stylistics. In C. Malcolm & J. Alison (Eds.), *The Routledge handbook of forensic linguistics* (pp. 487–508). Routledge.

Moeketsi, R. H. (1998). Statements about Sesotho questions used in the South African courtroom. *South African Journal of African Languages, 18*(3), 72–77.

Moeketsi, R. H. (1999a). Discourse structure in a criminal trial of a magistrate's court. *South African Journal of African Languages, 19*, 30–38.

Moeketsi, R. H. (1999b). Some observations on answers to courtroom questions. *South African Journal of African Languages, 19*, 237–244.

Naerssen, V. M. (2012). Faked or truthful second language proficiency: Assessing claims. In S. Tomblin, N. MacLeod, R. Sousa-Silva, & M. Coulthard (Eds.), *Proceedings of the international association of forensic linguists' tenth biennial conference* (pp. 306–314). Centre for Forensic Linguistics.

Ralarala, K. M., Kaschula, H. R., & Heydon, G. (Eds.). (2019). *New frontiers in forensic linguistics: Themes and perspectives in language and the law in Africa and beyond*. African Sun Media.

Shuy, W. R. (2001a). DARE's role in linguistic profiling. *Dictionary of American Regional English Newsletter*, 00–10. Retrieved from https://dare.wisc.edu/dare-newsletters/

Shuy, W. R. (2001b). Discourse analysis in the legal context. In D. Schiffrin, D. Tannen, & H. Hamilton (Eds.), *The handbook of discourse analysis* (pp. 437–452). Blackwell.

Shuy, W. R. (2002a). Breaking into language and the law: The trial of the insider linguist. In E. J. Alatis, E. H. Hamilton, & A.-H. Tan (Eds.), *Linguistics, language, and the professions: Education, journalism, law, medicine, and technology* (pp. 67–80). Georgetown University Press.

Shuy, W. R. (2002b). To testify or not to testify. In J. Cotterill (Ed.), *Language in the legal process* (pp. 03–18). Palgrave Macmillan.

Shuy, W. R. (2006). *Linguistics in the courtroom: A practical guide*. Oxford University Press.

Solan, L. M. (2002). The Clinton scandal: Some legal lessons from linguistics. In J. Cotterill (Ed.), *Language in the legal process* (pp. 180–195). Macmillan.

Stygall, G. (2010). Legal writing: Complexity complex documents/average and not-so-average readers. In M. Coulthard & A. Johnson (Eds.), *The Routledge handbook of forensic linguistics* (pp. 51–65). Routledge.

Tiersma, M. P. (2002). The language and law of product warnings. In J. Cotterill (Ed.), *Language in the legal process* (pp. 54–72). Palgrave Macmillan.

Wachal, R. S. (1966). *Linguistic evidence, statistical inference and disputed authorship* (Unpublished PhD dissertation). University of Wisconsin, Wisconsin.

CHAPTER 4

Cameroon Courtroom Discourse Analysis

Introduction

In three years of fieldwork, I observed courtroom discourse in Cameroon Courts of First Instance using a non-participant observation guide. The illiteracy of the adult population has prompted me to transcribe court discourse involving lay-litigants. The transcribed court cases are analysed using two approaches of Discourse Analysis (DA): the Speech Act Theory (SAT) and the Interactional Sociolinguistics (IS) principles of participants' background knowledge. Actually, I analysed 37 court cases involving lay-litigants to identify the speech acts used in the circumstances of languages barrier and linguistic inequality. This analysis also allows me to determine the language problems lay-litigants encounter during judicial proceedings. Therefore, this chapter presents and analyses 37 court discourse collected in the Courts of First Instance of Buea, Bafoussam, and Ngaoundéré, meanwhile, Yaoundé and Douala.

Research Methodology

In this study, I followed the qualitative research method. Qualitative research is an iterative process in which improved understanding of the scientific community is achieved by making new significant distinctions resulting from getting closer to the phenomenon studied (Aspers & Corte, 2019). In other words, qualitative research involves the collection and

E. M. K. Dissake, *Language and Legal Proceedings*,
https://doi.org/10.1007/978-3-030-76349-7_4

study of empirical materials, what people say and do in specific places and institutions (Denzin & Lincoln, 2005; Goodwin & Horowitz, 2002). The qualitative research method is an effective way to explore new and untouched areas of study like Cameroon courtroom discourse. The qualitative approach allows me to collect and analyse the speech act of court participants. In fact, qualitative research enables researchers to give meaning to human behaviour (Dornyei, 2007).

For the research design, I followed Walliman (2011) descriptive and evaluative research designs. Descriptive research design main instrument of data collection is observation. In this design, the researcher observes a setting to determine its norms and the exception. Evaluative research design deals with complex social issues. It aims at getting facts on a societal issue and makes sense out of it. This design entails a series of investigation steps to evaluate the social issues of a given setting. The results obtained from the evaluation are often used to propose solutions to societal problems. The descriptive and evaluative research designs concede with my research objective (observe courtroom discourse and study the speech act of the court participants).

I collected courtroom discourse through non-participant observation. Bogdan (1972) defined observation as research characterised by a prolonged period of intense social interaction between the researcher and the subjects, in the milieu of the latter, during which time, data, in the form of field notes, are unobtrusively and systematically collected. And Kumar (2011) suggested that non-participant observation is when a researcher does not participate in the activities of a group, but remains an inactive spectator, observing and listening to the activities and drawing conclusions (Kumar, 2011, p. 134). I chose the non-participant observation method of data collection because I did not participate in the court debates. Court participants were legal professionals (judges, state councils, lawyers, and clerks) and litigants (accused, plaintiffs, and witness).

It is worth noting that anthropologists use the term 'Unobtrusive Observation', which Bernard (2006) described as a research activity were researchers join or pretend to join, some group and secretly record data about people in the group (p. 455). However, in this work, I favoured the appellation non-participant observation rather than unobtrusive observation for two reasons. One, I did not secretly attend the court proceedings, but I obtained due permission from Courts of First Instance presidents. And two, as widely discussed by Bernard (2006), the term unobtrusive observation raises tough ethical questions, and I share his views. For instance, it is unethical to take note during court discourse without informing the court President.

The observation was carried out in natural settings (courtrooms). I did not participate (nor did I intervene) in any given activity during the observation sessions. I used an observation guide. The guide was divided into four parts: introductory information, court discourse, participant description, and researcher comments. In the first part, the introductory note, I entered the setting location, the date of the observation, the observation number, the time, the number, and roles of participants. I also provided the accusation levied on the accused person. In the descriptive section, I described the lay-litigants (mostly accused, plaintiff, and witness) by stating their sex, age, and estimated literacy level (the literacy levels were measure through language performance). In the third part, the court discourse, I noted down the discourse between the legal professionals and the litigants. And in the last section, the researcher comments, I wrote down instances of linguistics infelicity, use of illocutionary acts, and judicial misconduct.

Since Cameroon is a bilingual and bijural nation, data were collected in both Common law (English-speaking zones) and Civil law (French-speaking zones) districts. In fact, primary data were collected in the Courts of First Instance of Yaoundé, Douala, Bafoussam, Ngaoundéré[1] (all Civil law districts), and Buea (a Common law district). It is worth noting that Buea, Bafoussam, and Ngaoundéré are semi-urban areas, whereas Yaoundé and Douala (the political and economic capitals, respectively) are urban areas. To this effect, I recorded the use of national languages in the Courts of First Instance of Buea, Bafoussam, and Ngaoundéré, meanwhile, Yaoundé and Douala court discourses were conducted only in official languages as seen in the table below (Table 4.1):

Compared to urban areas, in semi-urban areas, the population literacy rate is lower. This is the reason why I registered the use of national languages like Pidgin English, Fulfulde, and Bamenjou/Ghomala' in the Courts of First Instance of Buea, Bafoussam, and Ngaoundéré, but Yaoundé and Douala recorded a 100% of French language.

Regarding the distribution of the data, 30% of the transcribed court cases came from Buea, 27% from Yaoundé, 19% from Douala, 13% from

[1] I also visited Dschang Court of First Instance, but I did not include its court cases in the analysis because the discourses were similar to what obtained in Bafoussam.

Table 4.1 Court discourse languages

Courts of first instance of:	*English (%)*	*French (%)*	*National languages (%)*
Buea	56	0	44
Douala	0	100	0
Yaoundé	0	100	0
Bafoussam	0	67	33
Ngaoundéré	0	83	17

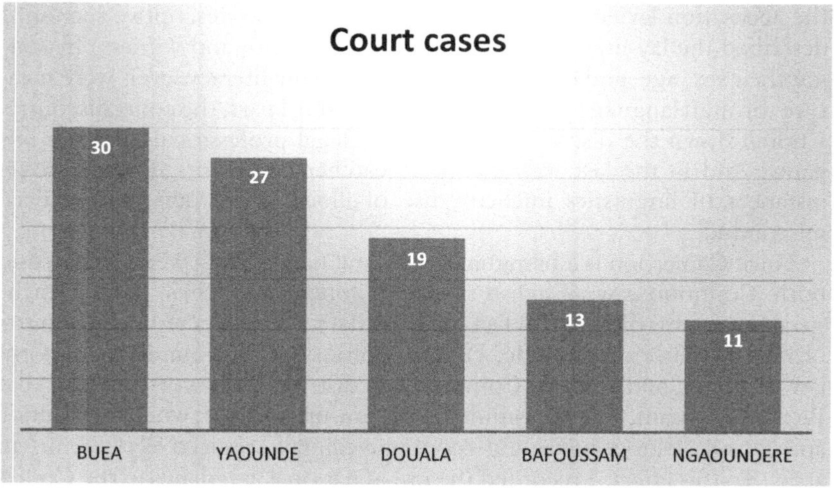

Fig. 4.1 Court cases

Bafoussam, and 11% from Ngaoundéré. The chart below illustrates this distribution (Fig. 4.1).

In addition to the absence of national language in urban areas court, I also noted the absence of court interpreters in those areas. Actually, out of the five courts visited, interpreters were only present in two courts: Bafoussam and Ngaoundéré. These interpreters were interpreting from official languages to national languages. In the Ngaoundéré Court of First Instance, the interpreter was mainly translating from French to Fulfulde and vice versa. It is also important to note that Bafoussam and Ngaoundéré had only one court interpreter each. Thus, a single interpreter worked from the beginning to the end of court sessions. One court session can last for ten (10) hours, and a session count at least 20 trials (a trial can last for 50 minutes).

I also recorded various prosecution motives throughout the research, some of which were child abuse, theft, scam, absence of national ID cards, land disputes, robbery, absence of residence permit, fraud, threat, infringement, aggression, embezzlement, destruction, and so on. Of all these offences the most recurrent were theft and land disputes.

Linguistics Framework: Discourse Analysis

In the field of Applied Linguistics, discourse has been studied under the frame of Discourse analysis (DA). DA is the study of texts, whether spoken or written, long or short, and is interested in the connection linking texts and the contexts in which they emerge and function (McCarthy et al., 2010, p. 53). Eggins and Slade (1997) identified various approaches to DA: Conversational Analysis, Interactional Sociolinguistics, Speech Act Theory, and so on. The chosen approach in this study is the Speech Act Theory (SAT); however, a snippet of the Interactional Sociolinguistics (IS) approach will be used at a certain point of our analysis.

Interactional Sociolinguistics (IS) a discourse analysis approach propounded by Gumperz. In 1982 Gumperz published two research works where he defined Interactional Sociolinguistics (IS) as the interface between discourse and pragmatics and/or between language use and context. Other researchers defined IS as the study of language use by people in face-to-face interactions. During face-to-face interactions, word or sentence meanings are always related to the context of the interaction. Thus, words meaning are most often embedded in context. Even though IS focuses more on interlocutors, it also studies how words are related to their contexts and how sentence production and reception subsequently influences interactions (Jürgen, 2011).

IS' point of departure was institutional communication. Miscommunication in institutional milieus can result in a wrong conclusion. For instance, because of miscommunication, someone may be found unintelligible, impolite, or insincere. Indeed, during institutional communications like job interviews, police interviews, and courtroom discourse, gatekeepers (authorities) expect people from different backgrounds to communicate using institutional conventions. For instance, Gumperz (2001) analysed the interview of a candidate applying for a paid traineeship. His analysis demonstrated the devastating effect of miscommunication in institutions.

It is sad to see how people are being rejected only because they do not succeed to follow a certain standard of communication (institutional conventions). Institutions possess interactional conventions which are strongly kept and cherished by gatekeepers. Those gatekeepers are prompt in condemning people whose languages do not conform to the institution's convention, whereas sociolinguistic studies always take into consideration language at the macro and micro levels.

The IS principle of identifying speakers' background knowledge of institutional codes of conduct (professional jargon and practices) will be used to analyse courtroom discourse in order to demonstrate that legal professionals, to a certain extent, do not take into consideration the linguistics and legal knowledge of lay-litigants. Most often, this omission let to the rejection of litigants' declarations during trials.

However, the major DA approach used in this study is the Speech Act Theory (SAT). Many years ago, John Austin gave a series of lectures inspired by Williams James' lectures. In 1962, those lectures were published in a book titled 'how to do things with words'. In this book, Austin's analysis of speaker utterances included: the meaning of words/sentences uttered, the intention of the speaker, and the effect of the utterances on the hearer. This analysis marked the creation of the Speech Act Theory (SAT). In SAT, languages and utterances are not only seen as modules used to describe the world, but also as modules through which one can express feelings, promise, condemnation, requests, judgement, and so on (Virbel, 2015). Another scholar who contributed to the development of this theory through his publications was Austin's student, John Searle. John Searle argued that "to speak a language is to perform speech acts, acts such as making statements, giving orders, asking questions or making promises [...] all linguistic communication involves linguistic (speech) acts" (Searle, 1975, p. 16).

According to Searle, when performing a speech act, a speaker either makes a statement, gives a command, or makes a request or promise. In other words, SAT enables us to see speeches not only from a linguistics perspective but also from a cultural, psychological, and social perspective. In addition, SAT stipulate that words do not only 'say' something, but they also 'do' things. This is the reason why the theory is termed 'speech' 'act'.

Austin (1962) divided the speech act into two categories, the Constatives and the Performatives. The Performatives were further divided into three acts: locutionary, illocutionary, and perlocutionary. The second, the illocutionary act, is considered the core of the Performative. This research will use the Performative act of the SAT to analyse Cameroon court discourse. To be more precise, two aspects of the Performatives act will be used: The illocutionary sub-categories and the Felicity condition.

Felicity Conditions

Felicity conditions are conditions necessary for the success of a speech act. Austin (1962) presented the Felicity conditions as such:

(A.1) There must exist an accepted conventional procedure having a certain conventional effect, that procedure to include the uttering of certain words by certain persons in certain circumstances, and further,
(A.2) the particular persons and circumstances in a given case must be appropriate for the invocation of the particular procedure invoked.
(B.1) The procedure must be executed by all participants both correctly and.
(B.2) completely.
(Γ.1) Where, as often, the procedure is designed for use by persons having certain thoughts or feelings, or for the inauguration of certain consequential conduct on the part of any participant, then a person participating in and so invoking the procedure must in fact have those thoughts or feelings, and the participants must intend so to conduct themselves, and further (Γ.2) must actually so conduct themselves subsequently. (pp. 14–15)

In general, all these conditions stipulate that in a speech act, the speaker should know the language of use, the rules of the language (phonetics, morphology, syntax, semantics, and pragmatics), be sincere and prepared to fulfil future responsibilities. Etsuko (2006) termed these conditions as the 'Conventionality, Actuality, and Intentionality of speech situations' (p. 07).

- Conventionality condition

Conventionality is placed under conditions A.1 and A.2 of Austin's Felicity conditions and a violation of these conditions is described as a 'misinvocation' (Austin, 1962, p. 18). This condition requires that speech acts must be in languages that both parties (speaker and hearer) understand and properly use. In other words, a speaker speech should make sense to the hearer. Another element of the Conventionality condition is the hierarchy (i.e. institutional codes of conduct). In a speech act situation, speakers should endeavour to respect the institutional codes of conduct for their speeches to be understood and accepted.

Of the 37 court cases transcribed, 32% showed evidence of Conventionality violation of language use and legal codes of conduct. In many instances, legal authorities questioned in official languages and lay-litigants answered in the national languages like Pidgin English, Fulfulde, or Ghomala. The inappropriate response of litigants during judicial proceedings are often regarded as dilatory tactics, that is, the act of not answering disturbing questions to avoid incriminating oneself. The Felicity conditions section aims to determine if litigants' inappropriate answers were a consequence of the language barrier or were just mere dilatory tactics.

In case 3 (three) of the observation guide, a man aged 40 was accused of money disruption in a microfinance where he worked. During his trial in the Court of First Instance of Buea, the judge presented his crimes and the eventual penalties in the English language[2]:

1. J: /presents the accusation and the corresponding condemnation in English/
2. AC: (.)
3. J: you don understand weti I just tok? < *did you understand what I just said?*>
4. AC: No sir.
5. J: You hear but you no understand. All the big book mean say (…) < *you heard but you didn't understand. In fact, this is what I said …*>

As seen in line 2, the accused remained silent after the judge's speech. The judge then asked, in Pidgin English, if he understood what he said, the accused answered 'no'. Indeed, the judge switched to Pidgin English

[2] The appendix identifies and describes the abbreviations and conventions used in the court extracts.

to help the accused who could not understand English.[3] However, the accused was neither a Pidgin English speaker as seen in the extract below:

8. AC: The cashier tok say yi don ova helep me and yi no fit 'saisir' the
9. money for me. < *The cashier said he's already helped me enough, he could not get the money for me again*>
10. J: Say weti? <*Sorry*>
11. AC: Yi say yi fit 'saisir' me money again. < *He said that could not get the money for me again*>
12. J: Yi mean say weti? Person fit helep yi? < *What does he mean by that? can someone help him?*>
13. O: {'Saisir' mean say type for machine}
14. J: So you no go ever pay the two million? <*So, you will never reimburse the money?*>
15. AC: How I go do pay wey them lock me for prison since. <*Where will I find the money in prison*>
16. SC: when your big man go leave, na you di be in control? < *When your boss was gone, did you stay in control?*>
17. AC: yes
18. SC: why you no tokam? You be get shortage for that time? <*Did you have shortage during that period* >
19. AC: Yes.
20. SC: Did you acknowledge it?
21. AC: Yes.
22. SC: Time wey you go police station you mek statement and you signam
23. no? <*When you were in the police station you made declarations that you signed* >
24. AC: Yes
25. SC: /she send the statement to the AC/ do you recognize it?
26. AC: I have never seen it!
27. SC: But this is your signature /showing the statement to the AC/
28. AC: 'je n'ai jamais dit ça, moi je n'ai jamais dit ça!' <*I have never said it*>
29. J: Speak in Pidgin!
30. AC: I no tokam. How I fit tok say I go pay 3 million from my salary?

[3] The Receptive Illocutionary Speech Acts of the legal authorities will be discussed in the upcoming sections.

31. That I gain how much? <*I have not said it. How can I say that I will take 3 million* from *my salary? How much is my salary?*>
32. SC: So na the officer that wey yi by force you for tokam sign? You don di
33. tok about 2 million, why you di tok about 3 million for police station. <*So, it is the police officer who forced you to sign those declarations? So, why did you talk of 3 million instead of 2 million?*>
34. AC: They di 'forcer' me for police for tok 3 million. < *The police officers made me say 3 million* >

In many instances, the accused used French words like 'saisir' (to type) and 'forcer' (to force), but, the judge didn't understand those words. In line 28, the accused did not limit himself to a single French word but uttered a whole sentence in French this annoyed the judge who ordered him to use pidgin (a language he, the judge, understood). In fact, the accused was a French speaker compelled to defend himself in Pidgin English. Because of his French language background, the accused violated the Conventionality condition in lines 8, 11, 28, and 34.

In case 23 of our observation guide, a woman sued her father-in-law in the Court of First Instance of Bafoussam. The judge started the trial in French and later on realised that the plaintiff does not understand French.

1. J: Pour quelle raison avez-vous saisi le tribunal? <*why are you in court?*>
2. PL: (.)
3. J: Elle s'exprime en quelle langue? \s'adressant au TD\ <*What language does she speak?\ addressing the TD*>
4. TD: Bamenjou
5. J: \fais signe à l'interprète\ <asked the interpreter to translate>[4]

After the judge's inquiry in line 1, the plaintiff remained silent. The judge understood that the plaintiff certainly did not understand French. Indeed, the plaintiff's first language was Bamenjou[5] as indicated by the witness in line 4. Thus, the judge requested the assistance of the interpreter in line 5. The interpreter translated the judge's questions in

[4] Each time the judge looked at the interpreter, it means she/he can translate.

[5] Ghomala' is the autonym and Bamenjou an alternate name. Ghomala' is a Cameroon national language spoken in the West Region by the Bamileke tribe (Eberhard et al., 2019).

Bamenjou and the plaintiff's answered in French. Anyway, the language performance of the plaintiff was not the most interesting element of this court case. What caught my attention was the conduct of the interpreter. Actually, the interpreter violated the Conventionality condition by transgressing the code of conduct of the court as illustrated in the extract below.

6. IN: \traduit la question du J en Bamenjou\ <*translates the judge's question into Bamenjou*>
7. PL: \répond en Bamenjou\ <*answers in Bamenjou*>
8. IN: \chuchote la traduction française à l'oreille du J\ <*whispers the French translation in the judge's ears*>
9. J: Votre enfant à quel âge? <How old is your child>
10. TD: \traduit la question en Bamenjou\ <*translates the question into* Bamenjou>
11. PL: \répond en Bamenjou\ <*answers in Bamenjou*>
12. IN: \chuchote la traduction française à l'oreille du J\ <*whispers the French translation in the judge's ears* >
13. J: Qu'a laissé votre mari, que vous revendiquez aujourd'hui? <*what did your late husband left, that you are claiming today?*>
14. IN: \traduit en Bamenjou\ <*translates into Bamenjou*>
15. PL: \répond en Bamenjou\ <*answers in Bamenjou*>
16. IN: \chuchote la traduction française à l'oreille du J\ <*whispers the French translation in the judge ears* >

Each time the interpreter translated the plaintiff's answers to the judge, he whispered the translation in the judge's ear in such a way that no one else could hear him. This way of doing is in violation of the court codes of conduct. Indeed, legal code of conduct demands that all parties should hear the translation of the interpreter in order to call the judge's attention in case of a miscarriage. But no parties heard the interpreter's translation, so, no one could attest to the adequacy of the translation. Thus, the plaintiff will receive a verdict without the assurance that her testimonies were properly translated.

Another legal authority who violated the court codes of conduct was the state counsel of case 1 (one) of the observation guide. This case involves a woman aged 50 who sued a young man in the Court of First Instance of Buea because he impregnated her daughter. Because the plaintiff could not speak English, the defence lawyer examined her in Pidgin

English. Yet, even the use of Pidgin English did not solve the language problem of the plaintiff.

1. DL: Na you bi the real mami for Grace? <*Are you the mother of Grace?*>
2. PL: No
3. DL: You sabi day wey them born Grace? < *Do you know the date of birth of Grace?*>
4. PL: No
5. DL: You no even sabi anything about Grace. You wan na ele…
6. Yi fit cam helep you for work. < *You don't know anything about Grace, all you care about is having her come and help you at home.*>
7. PL: Yes
8. DL: Na you personally pay Grace yi school fee? <*Were you the one paying Grace school fees?*>
9. PL: Yes
10. DL: Na weti be the school fee? <*How much was the school fee?*>
11. PL: I no. Na my daughter bi payam. <*I don't know, my daughter was the one paying.*>
12. DL: You bi mek agreement withi di man? /pointing at the accused/ <*Do you have an agreement with this man?*>
13. PL: Yes
14. DL: So ya worry nan a say the person wey them accus'am no follow the agrement. The
15. person wey them accus'am no bi gi you small tin after yi gi Grace belle. <*So, your problem is that he didn't respect the agreement. But, didn't he give you something after having impregnated Grace?*>
16. PL: Yes
17. DL: You no say for 19 Grace don correct for mek yi own decision. <*you know that at 19 years old Grace is already capable of making her own decision*>
18. PL: I no sabi … weti I want na 110000frs <*Me, I do not know. All I want is 110000frs*>
19. DL: The person wey them accus'am no go gi you even 1 franc. <*The person you accuse is not going to give you anything*>
20. SC: /repeat what the DL said to the plaintiff/
21. DL: Grace be born na for Oct. 2016, no bi so? < *Grace give birth on October 2016?*>
22. PL: Yes

23. SC: Mamy this lawyer say you nova spend nothing for Grace, na true? <*Madam, this lawyer is saying that you have never done something for grace*>
24. PL: I don spend. <*I did*>
25. SC: Explain
26. PL I don do plenty thins. I di buy plantains, bedshit them, matrass …<*I bought many things like plantains, bedsheet, matrass …*>
27. DL: Is the state counsel re-examining the plaintiff? Because he is bringing
28. in new argument.

As seen in the above extract, the plaintiff had many difficulties answering the defence lawyer's questions. For instance, in lines 9 and 11, I realise that she did not understand the meaning of the question 'Na you personally pay Grace yi school fee?' Seeing the difficulties that the plaintiff was going through, the state counsel gave her some elements to thwart the argument of the defence lawyer. Nevertheless, the state counsel did not have the right to do that; actually, that was a violation of the code of conduct of the court.

The clerk of case 11 of the observation guide also violated the Conventionality condition by transgressing the code of conduct of the court.

1. J: The accused has been found guilty of phone stealing and of moving
2. without a national ID meanwhile, he is 20 years old.
3. CK: Court don find you guilty, beg mek court no ova punish you. <*You have been found guilty, ask that your sentence be reduced*>
4. AC: I beg mek court no ova punish me /he kneels down/ < *I ask the court to reduce my sentence*>
5. J: Stand up. Sentence count 1: convict shall pay a fine of 30000frs, count
6. 2: convict shall pay to the plaintiff an amount of 70000frs and to the
7. government 44000frs.
8. CK: /He repeat the sentence in Pidgin English/

Knowing that the accused could not understand the English words of the judge, the clerk decided to help the accused by translating the judge's utterances in Pidgin English as seen in lines 3 and 8. In normal circumstances, an interpreter should have been present in the court in order to translate the judge's utterances. The law prohibits members of a court from playing the role of an interpreter at hearings. However, the clerk was receptive to the linguistics problems of the accused.

Nonetheless, the most interesting legal codes of conduct violation is seen in case 28 of the observation guide. In the Ngaoundéré Court of First Instance, a defence lawyer requested for the resumption of debates at the end of the hearings.

1. AD: Nous demandons la réouverture des débats. <*we are requesting for the resumption of debates*>
2. J: Pourquoi? Nous avons déjà clos les débats. <*why? we have already closed the debates*>
3. AD: Mon client n'avait pas compris les trois options qui lui avaient été
4. offertes à l'ouverture du procès. <*my client did not understand the three options presented to him at the beginning of the trial*>
5. J: Comment ça? J'avais répété chacune des options plusieurs fois et il
6. avait choisi la première option. N'est-ce pas? /au AD/ <*how? I repeated each of the options several times and he chose the first one*>
7. AC: Oui, mais je n'avais pas bien compris. <*yes, but I did not understand those options*>
8. J: J'avais répété les options combien de fois? <*how many times did I repeat those options?*>
9. AC: Trois fois. <*three times*>
10. J: Et alors? Vous ne comprenez pas français? <*so what is the problem? don't you understand French?*>
11. AC: Je ne suis pas habitué aux choses-ci. Je ne savais pas ce que les options là signifiaient. <*I am not used to judicial proceedings. I didn't know the meaning of those options*>
12. J: Ok. Nous rouvrons les débats. <*Ok. We shall resume the debates*>
13. AD: Merci <*thank you.*>
14. J: Vous étiez d'abord où /blague/ <*where were you at the beginning?* > */joke/*
15. AD: C'est maintenant qu'il a fait appel à moi. Il s'est rendu compte que
16. les choses n'allaient pas à son avantage. < *He called for me when he realized that he was in trouble*>

The request of the lawyer in line 1 is in complete violation of article 3 subsection 2 of the Criminal Procedure Code, which states that:

> (2) Nullity as referred to subsection (1) of this section shall not be overlook be raised at any stage of the criminal proceedings by any of the parties and shall be raised by the trial court of its own motion. (Criminal Procedure Code of the Republic of Cameroon, 2005a)

Moreover, article 170 subsection 2(d) adds that if the litigant cannot immediately call a lawyer, he is free to do so at any time before the investigation is closed (Criminal Procedure Code of the Republic of Cameroon, 2005b).

According to these articles, the accused was not allowed to call a lawyer at the end of the inquiry. However, the judge approved the request of the defence lawyer. This approval was certainly due to the argument of the accused who admitted he had trouble grasping the legal jargon of the judge. Therefore, I can argue that the judge considered the poor language competence of the accused who in normal circumstances, had to be assisted by an interpreter throughout the proceeding.

Case 21 took place in the Court of First Instance of Yaoundé. In this case, the accused did not have a lawyer and had to play two roles: witness and defence lawyer, yet he had no experience and therefore performed poorly in each of those roles.

/Le J demande au AC s'il a des questions, et le AC se met à poser des questions au TP3/ < *The J asked the AC if the latter has questions, and the AC started interrogating the TP3.*>

65. AC: Ou étais-tu quand je détruisais les champs? <*Where were you when I was destroying the farm?*>
66. TP3: Sur le terrain. <*On the land*>
67. AC: Mais tu viens de dire que tu étais chez toi quand tu as entendu des
68. cris. Donc, tu étais au champs et chez toi en même temps. <*But you have just said that you were in your house when you heard shouting. So you were in the farm and at your place at the same time*>
69. J: Quelle est la question? <*What is the question*>
70. AC: Où étais-tu? <*Where were you?*>
71. TP3: Sur le terrain. <*On the land*>

/le AC passe à la bar/ <*the accused goes to the bar*>

72. AC: Mr. le president /il s'adresse au J avec l'intention de faire une plaidoirie/ < *He addresses the J with the intention to plead (to start a pleading)*>
73. J: Non. Non↑ <*No. No*>
74. AD: Mr. (...) je pose les questions et vous répondez. Dites-nous ce qui
75. s'est passé. <*Sir, I ask questions and you answer. Tell us what happened*>
76. AC: /raconte les faits sans toutefois parler des faits de destruction/ <*tells the facts without mentioning the part concerning the destruction*>
77. AD: Mr. (...) nous parlons des faits de destruction et non d'autre chose. <*Sir, we are talking about the destruction and nothing else*>

When the accused agreed to examine the third prosecution witness, he hence played the role of a defence lawyer. The accused had no experience, and that's the reason why he didn't ask good questions in lines 67 and 68. Apart from being a poor examiner/lawyer, the accused was also a poor witness as seen in line 72. Therefore, the accused violated Conventionality conditions in both role plays.

As demonstrated in the court extracts presented in this subsection, the Conventionality conditions were violated in two ways: the language use and the legal codes of conduct. The chart below illustrates the analysis of the Conventionality violations (Fig. 4.2):

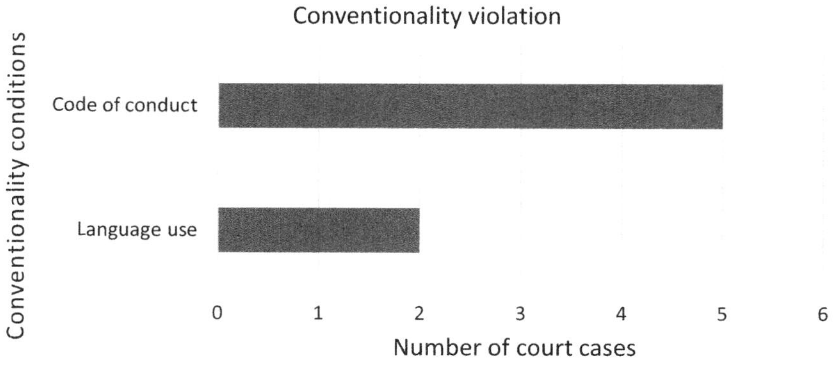

Fig. 4.2 Conventionality violation

The most violated Conventionality condition was the legal codes of conduct; however, the language use condition was also violated. Many lay-litigants felt more comfortable using Pidgin English as seen in cases 1, 3, and 11, and others preferred using national languages as seen in case 23. By expressing themselves in their preferred (first) languages, litigants demonstrated their inability to hear and speak official languages. Therefore, lay-litigant's violations of the Conventionality condition cannot be regarded as dilatory tactics, but as evidence of the language barrier.

Nevertheless, instances of violations of court code of conducts surpassed the language use violation. What is interesting is that the legal codes of conduct were mostly violated by legal professionals, as seen in the chart below (Fig. 4.3).

Undeniably, litigants violated court codes of conduct because of their poor knowledge of judicial techniques and rules. However, the court codes of conduct were mainly violated by legal professionals. The analysis revealed that legal professionals' violations were due to their receptive attitude towards the illiteracy of lay-litigants.

For instance, in case 1, the state counsel violated the court code of conduct because he wanted to help a plaintiff who was persecuted by a

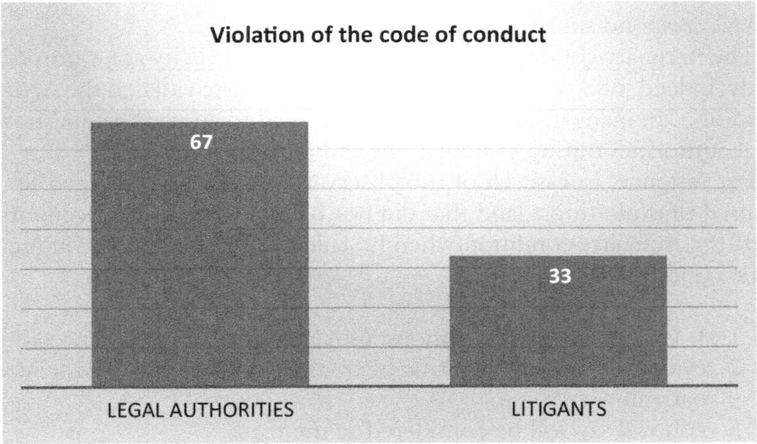

Fig. 4.3 Violation of the code of conduct

defence lawyer during the cross-examination phase. In case 11, the clerk helped the accused by translating the judge words in Pidgin English when she realised that the accused did not understand English language. In case 28, the defence lawyer violated the court code of conduct when requesting for the re-opening of the debates almost at the end of the trial. The lawyer demonstrated that the previous debates were unfair on account that his client's language competence was not taken into consideration by the court. And in case 23, a court interpreter whispered in the ears of the judge instead of talking aloud in such a way that all parties listen to his translations. The analysis of the interviews (in Chap. 4) will allow us to understand that the interpreter behaved in this way because he did not receive proper training. However, before getting into the interviews, let us first present the second type of Felicity condition violated in Cameroon Courts of First Instance, the Actuality conditions.

- Actuality conditions

Actuality is placed under conditions B.I and B.2 of Austin's Felicity conditions; a violation of these conditions is described as a 'misexecutions' (Austin, 1962, p. 18). These conditions stipulate that when a speaker utters a speech in a specific manner, the hearer should acknowledge/behave/respond subsequently.

The Actuality condition was the most violated Felicity condition of this study; indeed, 68% of the transcribed court discourse violated the Actuality condition. In many instances, lay-litigants failed to answer the questions of legal authorities during examinations and cross-examinations.

For instance, in case 16 of the observation guide, a man aged 86 was accused of exploiting a land that did not belong to him. The accused violated the Actuality condition when he failed to respond to the judge and clerk's questions.

1. J: Pa, you have three options: remain silence, give evidence, or give
2. evidence on oath. Remember that if you give evidence on oath all what
3. you will say will be considered as the truth.
4. AC: (.)
5. J: Lawyer, he is your client, what do you choose?
6. DL: Third option.
7. CK: Pa you wish to talk in which language?

8. AC: (.)
9. CL: You want talk for which language, Pidgin or English? <*You want to talk in which language?*>
10. AC: Pidgin.

At the beginning of each trial, judges ask accused persons to choose one option among the three that the law provides. Alas, the accused of this case failed to choose any of the three options. In line 5, the judge was then forced to ask his lawyer to choose for him. In line 8, the accused did not also respond to the clerk's question. In fact, the accused violated the Actuality condition by not responding to the legal authority questions. But the accused's response in line 10 enabled me to understand that his silence was due to the language barrier. Indeed, the accused is not an English speaker, but rather a Pidgin English speaker.

In the Courts of First Instance of Bafoussam and Ngaoundéré, many lay-litigants spoke neither French nor English and still less Pidgin English; they spoke other national languages. This language barrier led to the violation of the Actuality condition in many cases. For instance, in case 26, the accused, aged 20, sued for the offence of theft, violated the Actuality condition when he failed to respond to the judge.

1. J: Le tribunal déclare Mr. (…) coupable de vol et d'absence de CNI, le
2. condamne à 38 mois de prison et à 80 mille franc d'amende ferme. Dix
3. jours pour exercer les droits de recours. < *The court declares Mr (…) guilty of theft and absence of CNI, sentences him to 38 months imprisonment, and a fine of 80 thousand francs. He has ten days to exercise the rights of recourse/appeal* >
4. AC: (.)
5. J: Tu as compris? <*Have you understood?* >
6. AC: (.)
7. J: Interprète <*interpreter*>
8. IN: /Traduit en fulfulde/ <*translate in Fulfulde*>
9. AC: /Répond en fulfulde/ <*answer in Fulfulde*>

The accused violated the Actuality condition in lines 4 and 6 because he did not understand French. Indeed, the accused demonstrated proficiency in Fulfulde[6] in lines 8 and 9. By chance, an interpreter assisted the accused by translating the judge's speech in Fulfulde.

English (2010) declared that some lay-litigants involved in judicial proceedings lie on their linguistic competence because they are ashamed of their limitations, and she called this 'Linguistics Bravado'. Most often, lay-litigants demonstrating linguistics bravado refuse the assistance of court interpreters. I registered some cases of linguistic bravado during court discourse.

In case 24 of the observation guide, a woman aged 60 sued a man in the Court of First Instance of Bafoussam. At the beginning of the trial, the judge realised that the plaintiff did not understand French. She then proposed the assistance of an interpreter, but the plaintiff refused.

1. J: Pour quelle raison êtes-vous devant la cours? <*Why are you in front of the court?*>
2. PL: Quoi? <*What?* >
3. J: Vous parlez quelle langue? On va vous aider à traduire. *What language do you speak? An interpreter will help you* >
4. PL: Je parle un peu français. <*I speak a bit of French*>
5. J: J'espère que vous allez vous en sortir. Vous êtes née où? <*I hope you will be able to make it. Where were you born?* >
6. PL: Ici <*Here*>
7. J: Où ici? <*here where?*>
8. PL: (.)
9. J: Vous êtes née en quelle année? < *When were you born?*>
10. PL: (.)
11. J: Vous avez quel âge? <*How old are you?* >
12. PL: 43 ans. <*43* >
13. J: Vous êtes sur? <*Are you sure?*> */ J is surprised because PL seems to be at least 60 years/*

In line 4, the plaintiff refused the assistance of an interpreter alleging that she speaks French. Actually, the plaintiff's performance in French was not as good as she claimed. In effect, the plaintiff failed to respond to the judge's questions in lines 8 and 10, and when she finally succeeded to answer some few questions, she made numerous mistakes as seen in line 6

[6] Fulfulde is a language of wider communication spoken in the three northern regions of Cameroon (Eberhard et al., 2019).

where she failed to situate her place of birth, and in line 12 where she gave a wrong age. In fact, the plaintiff violated the Actuality condition in lines: 6, 8, 10, and 12 because of her linguistic bravado.

Another lay participant who violated the Actuality condition because of linguistic bravado was the plaintiff of case 25, a man aged 50 who was asking for the custody of his children in the Court of First Instance of Bafoussam.

1. J: Pourquoi êtes-vous devant la cours aujourd'hui? <*Why are you in front of the court today?*>
2. PL: */The French of the PL is too rough, one can hardly get what he says/*
3. J: Mr., parlez de manière à ce qu'on puisse vous comprendre. Si vous ne
4. Pouvez pas le faire en français faites le en langue maternelle et on traduira. < *Sir, talk in such a way that we can get you. If you cannot do it in French, do it in your mother-tongue, someone will interpret*>
5. PL: /he continues using his imperfect French/
6. J: Vous êtes qui pour lui? <*who are you to him?*>
7. PL: Je suis la mère des enfants. < *I am the mother of the children*>
8. J: Vous êtes une femme ↑< *Are you a woman* ↑>

Noticing the poor language performance of the plaintiff, the judge suggested him to use his mother tongue for an interpreter to translate. The plaintiff refused to speak in his mother tongue and continued using his approximate/imperfect French throughout the trial. Because of his linguistic bravado, the plaintiff violated the actuality condition in various instances. In line 7, he called himself a woman meanwhile he is a man. This, of course, angered the judge who asked in a harsh tone if he was a woman.

Questioning is a common practice in courtrooms. Legal practitioners like lawyers, state counsels, and even judges have the duty to question litigants during the examination and cross-examination phases. These two phases are nightmares to many lay-litigants who often violate the Actuality conditions simply because they fail to answer simple yes/no questions. For instance, in case 20, the second accused person failed to appropriately respond to a yes-or-no question asked by the state counsel, in lines 5 and 7.

4. PR: Reconnaissez-vous avoir plaidé coupable? <*Do you acknowledge your guilty plea?*>

5. AC2: Mr. Le procureur, je ne sais même pas ce qui se passe. <*Mr. the state counsel, I don't even know what is going on*>
6. PR: Donc, vous contestez vos premières déclarations? <*So, you are contesting your first declarations?*>
7. AC2: Par exemple, ce qu'on dit là que j'ai dit que Mr. (…) a insulté le
8. Substitut, je n'ai pas dit ça. <*For example, I never said that Mr. (…) insulted the state counsel*>

In other instances, I observed lay-litigants who not only failed to answer yes-or-no questions but went as far as correcting legal authorities' questions. In the Court of First Instance of Yaoundé, a plaintiff corrected a defence lawyer during the cross-examination:

1. AD: Vous avez des attestations de succession? <*Do you have any attestation of succession*>
2. PL: Ce n'est pas ce type de questions que vous devez me poser. <*This is not the type of question you should be asking me*>
3. J: Répondez à la question. < *Answer the question*>

Actually, the defence lawyer wanted to know if the plaintiff had an attestation of succession. Instead of answering the question with a simple yes or no, the plaintiff said that the lawyer's question was inappropriate. The judge of this case also got angry and ordered the plaintiff to answer the lawyer's question.

I recorded other court cases where lay-litigants violated the Actuality conditions because they misinterpreted terms. Among such cases is case 2 of the observation guide where a man, aged 30, accused of embezzlement violated the Actuality condition because he falsified terms.

1. SC: Were you aware that your accomplice was in the police station under
2. Arrest?
3. AC: He did not tell me but I suspected.
4. SC: You knew that there was a money problem in the Agency?
5. AC: No
6. SC: You knew about the money problem?
7. AC: I knew about the issue of 60 million.
8. SC: You are not telling the truth. You knew that there was a shortage, true or false?
9. AC: I knew

From what we can read in lines 4 to 10, the accused person differentiated the term 'money problem' from 'money issue'. In all likelihood, for the accused, the term 'money problem' has a negative connotation, whereas the 'money issue' connotation is neutral. This is why in line 5, the accused denied being aware of a money problem but admitted that he knew about the money issue in line 7. Because of this misinterpretation, the accused violated the Actuality condition in lines 5 and 7. In effect, the response of the accused was not per the state counsel's questions. This, therefore, explains why the state counsel called the accused a liar in lines 8 and 9. However, as seen in the extract below, this was not the only instance were the poor definition of terms put the accused in trouble.

14. SC: Let me ask you this question. Who employed you in the agency?
15. AC: The board of directors.
16. SC: How often do you communicate with them?
17. AC: I don't speak directly to them.
18. SC: You are not answering my question. The court will not take into
19. consideration your allegations because you are not speaking the truth.

From what we can read in lines 16, 17, 18, and 19, the accused violated the Actuality condition when he failed to answer the state counsel's question. The accused talked of 'speaking' while the state counsel talked of 'communication'. This other violation annoyed the state counsel who told the accused that his testimonies will not be considered because he was not speaking the truth.

One more reason why lay-litigant violated the Actuality condition was because of the legal jargon. Indeed, the legal jargon used by legal professionals put many lay-litigants in difficult positions. For instance, in case 4, an alcohol trader aged 50 accused of embezzlement and judged in the Court of First Instance of Yaoundé, violated the Actuality condition when he failed to choose one option among the three presented by the clerk.

1. GR: Mr., trois options s'offrent à vous <*Sir, you have three options…*>/ *he quotes the three options using the legal jargon/*
2. AC: Je n'ai pas compris <*I did not understand*>
3. GR: Demandez à votre avocat <*Ask to your lawyer*>

/The accused does not have a lawyer. He therefore asks for help from the lawyers present in the hall. One of them advised him to choose the third option/.

4. *AC: /after Choosing the Third Options, he Starts with his Declarations/*

In line 2, the accused did not answer the clerk's questions and thus violated the Actuality condition. I realise that the accused violated the Actuality condition because he did not understand the legal jargon of the clerk. Sadly, he had neither a lawyer nor an interpreter to assist him. The accused ended up asking for the help of lawyers present in the hall even though those lawyers were paid to assist other litigants.

The accused of case 27 prosecuted in the Court of First Instance of Ngaoundéré also violated the Actuality condition because he did not understand a legal term.

10. J: Vous avez des témoins? <*Do you have witnesses?* >
11. AC: Oui j'ai beaucoup de photos. <*Yes I have many pictures*>
12. J: Non. Ce n'est pas ce que j'ai demandé. Je veux savoir si vous avez des
13. témoins? < *This is not was I am asking. I want to know if you have witnesses.*>

In law, the term 'witness' refers to a person who saw a crime or a person who was a victim of a crime. The accused did not know the definition of the word 'witness', which he mistook for 'evidence' (in French, 'preuve'). When the judge asked if he had a witness, instead of talking of a person, he talked of photos. By so doing, he violated the Actuality condition.

Further person who violated the Actuality condition because she did not understand the legal jargon was the plaintiff of case 5 of the observation guide. The plaintiff is a woman of 50 years who sued a man to the Court of First Instance of Yaoundé because he extorted her 3,550,000 francs CFA.

1. J: Vous constituez partie civile? <*Do you want to act as a civil party*?>
2. PL: Je ne comprends pas. <*I don't understand*>
3. J: Vous voulez être partie civile? <*Do you want to be a civil party*?>
4. PL: Je ne sais pas. <*I don't know*>

<*A lawyer in the hall went toward the plaintiff to give her the meaning of the term 'civil party'*>.

The plaintiff did not know that when you constitute yourself a 'civil party', you have the opportunity to propose the type of reparations you would like the court to order, this is the reason why she fails to answer the judge's questions in lines 2 and 4. By chance, a lawyer present in the hall helped her by defining the legal term. However, the lawyer who helped the plaintiff was not present in the court for her. Just like the accused of the preceding case, the plaintiff took advantage of the presence of someone else lawyer.

In the Court of First Instance of Yaoundé, an ex-tenant sued his landlord, a man, aged 50, for theft. During the first phase of the examination, the accused never succeeded to answer the defence lawyer questions, as seen in the extract below.

5. AD: Pouvez-vous nous situer? Quand exactement avez-vous commencé à
6. rembourser le loyer à Mr. (…)? <*Can you tell us when exactly you started reimbursing the rent of Mr. (…)?*>
7. AC: Au moment où j'ai eu l'apostat. < *At the moment I had the prostrate* >
8. AD: En 2016? <*In 2016?*>
9. AC: Quand je suis allé me soigner au village. < *When I went to get treatment in the village* >
10. AD: Dites-nous, est-ce que c'était en 2015 ou 2016? <*Tell us was it in 2015 or 2016?*>
11. AC: Quand j'étais déjà parti. <*When I was already away*>

The defence lawyer wanted to know the date the accused (his client) started reimbursing his former tenant's rent, but by three times, the accused failed to answer the lawyer's question. Because the examinee was his client, the lawyer did not get annoyed. However, the accused did not only violate the Actuality condition during the examination of his lawyer. He also did the same during the cross-examination of the state counsel.

23. PR: Aviez-vous un contrat de bail avec Mr. (…)? <*Do you have a lease agreement with Mr (…)?*>
24. AD: Non. <*No*>
25. AC: Oui. <*Yes*>

26. AD: /To his client/ Un contrat de bail signé? <*A signed lease?* >
27. AC: Oui, on avait causé. <*Yes, we have discussed*>
28. AD: Mais vous avez mis vos paroles par écrit? <*Did you write down your agreement*>
29. AC: Non, mais on s'était entendu. <*No, but we agreed*>
30. PR: Moi je veux voir un contrat de bail signé. <*I want to see a signed lease*>

The state counsel wanted to know if the accused and his ex-tenant had a lease outlining the terms of the contract. Unfortunately, the accused did not know the meaning of 'lease'. Therefore, the accused violated the Actuality condition in lines 27 and 29 when giving an inappropriate answer to the state counsel.

One more lay-litigant who violated the Actuality condition because of the difficulty of the legal jargon was the accused of case 30 of the Court of First Instance of Ngaoundéré. The accused, who was prosecuted under articles 74 and 100 of the Cameroon Penal Code, failed to understand the clerk's English.

1. GR: Vous êtes accusé d'avoir détenu du carburant frelaté, ceci en
2. connaissance ou non du danger dudit produit. En le faisant, vous violez
3. l'article 74 et 100 du Code Pénal < *You are accused of having held adulterated fuel, this with knowledge or not of the danger of the product. By doing so, you are violating article 74 and 100 of the Penal Code* >
4. J: Vous plaidez coupable ou non-coupable? <*You plead guilty or not guilty?*>
5. AC: Je n'ai pas compris <*I didn't understand*>

Obviously, the accused did not understand the clerk sentence in lines 1 to 3 because it contains an extract of the Cameroon Penal code. Moreover, the term 'adulterated fuel' is not very common among Cameroonians. Indeed, it is a term mostly used in legal discourse.

In sum, the above subsection exposed five main reasons why lay-litigants violated the Actuality condition:

1. Misinterpretation of terms
2. Legal jargon
3. Linguistics bravado

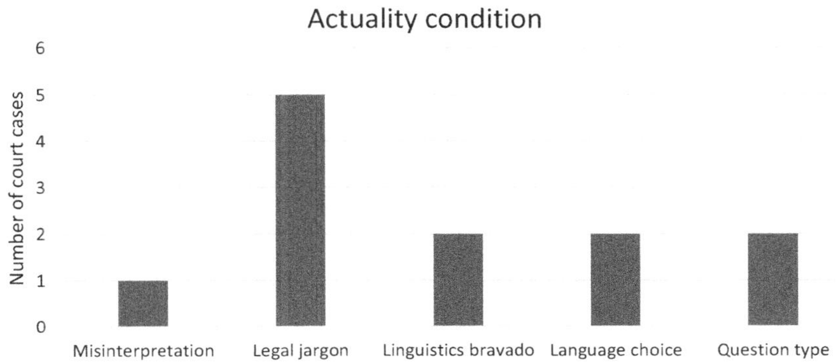

Fig. 4.4 Actuality condition

4. Language choice
5. Question types

Among these five reasons, the legal jargon registered the highest number of cases as seen in the chart below (Fig. 4.4).

From the above chart, the legal jargon was the motive that recorded the highest number of cases, linguistic bravado, language choice and question type, registered the same number of cases. The motive with the lowest number of cases was the misinterpretation of terms.

I will conclude the Felicity conditions sub topic with the chart below (Fig. 4.5):

The Conventionality and the Actuality conditions were violated in the transcribed court discourse. The Actuality condition was violated more than the Conventionality condition. However, in the analysis, I noted that lay-litigants violated the Felicity conditions because of the language barrier. The transcription demonstrated that the languages used in Cameroon Courts of First Instance (English and French) are scarcely known by litigants. Litigants were more proficient in national languages like Pidgin English and Fulfulde. Fortuitously, legal authorities were often receptive to the language problems of lay-litigants. This attitude prompted the use of an illocutionary act specific to Cameroon courtroom discourse, the Receptive Illocutionary Speech Act. This illocutionary sub-category will be discussed in the subsection below.

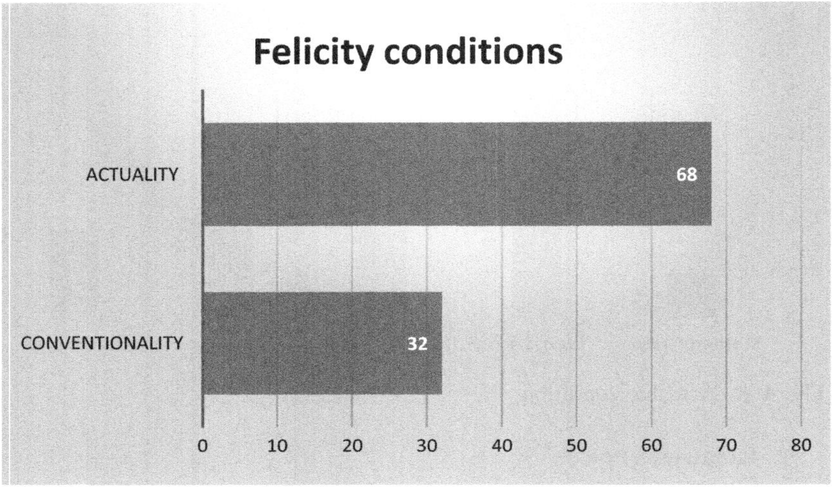

Fig. 4.5 Felicity conditions

Illocutionary Sub-categories

The illocutionary act is the action performed by the speaker when uttering a sentence and this act is closely related to the speaker's intentions. Austin (1965) stipulated that the illocutionary acts are speeches uttered by speakers with intention (keeping the motive in mind). This includes asking or answering a question, giving information, warning, announcing a verdict or intention, naming, appealing, criticising, and describing. Thus, Austin claimed that the illocutionary act is complete and carry some force. Austin (1962) divided the illocutionary act into five sub-categories: verdictives, exercitives, commissives, behabitives, and expositives.

Cameroon legal professionals like lawyers, state counsels, and judges used three illocutionary sub-categories (exercitives, verdictives, and behabitives) when criticising litigants and other legal authorities sometimes without considering their linguistics and legal knowledge (as required in the IS theory). However, I not only noted critics, but also observed a receptive attitude towards lay-litigants' language problems. The court cases presented below[7] are analysed using the illocutionary sub-categories and the feature of speakers' background knowledge (IS theory).

[7] Some of those court cases are also present in the Felicity conditions section.

- Verdictive acts

Verdictives are utterances meant for judgement. When issuing a judgement, a verdict, a condemnation, a warning, advice, a vote, an order, and so on, we talk of verdictive utterances. Thus, verdictive utterances are commonly used in courtrooms. In the extracts below, we observe a state counsel condemning the misconduct of a litigant. Indeed, in case 2 of the observation guide, a state counsel utters verdictive speeches to censured the slip-ups of the accused person.

1. SC: Were you aware that your accomplice was in the police station under
2. arrest
3. AC: He did not tell me but I suspected.
4. SC: You knew that there was a money problem in the agency?
5. AC: No
6. SC: You knew about the money problem?
7. AC: I knew about the issue of 60 million.
8. SC: You are not telling the truth. You knew that there was a shortage in the
9. agency, true or false?
10. AC: I knew
11. SC: You knew that your accomplice was in detention and you called him.
12. True or false?
13. AC: I knew it.
14. SC: let me ask you this question. Who employed you in the agency?
15. AC: The board of directors.
16. SC: How often do you communicate with them?
17. AC: I don't speak directly to them.
18. SC: You are not answering my question. The court will not take into
19. consideration your statements because you are not speaking the truth.

The state counsel's utterances in lines 8, 9, 18, and 19 are verdictive illocutionary acts. In lines 8 and 9, the state counsel reproved the accused when she said he wasn't telling the truth. In lines 18 and 19, the state counsel called the accused a liar. She added that the court will not consider the accused person declarations. In fact, the state council illocutionary verdictive act did not correspond the litigant linguistic abilities in the court language.

- Behabitive acts

This illocutionary act involves various speech types like apologies, congratulations, commends, condolences, curses, and challenges. Here, the speaker adopts an attitude or expresses his feelings to his hearer. When legal authorities wanted to expose their objection to other legal authorities and litigants, they used the behabitive act. For instance, in case 1 of the observation guide, a defence lawyer reproved a state counsel.

23. SC: Mamy this lawyer say you nova spend nothing for Grace, na true? <*Madam, this lawyer is saying that you have never done something for grace*>
24. PL: I don spend. <*I did*>
25. SC: Explain
26. PL: I don do plenty thins. I di buy plantains, bedshit them, matrass ...<*I bought many things like plantains, bedsheet, matrass ...*>
27. DL: Is the state counsel re-examining the plaintiff? Because he is bringing in new argument.

In every normal judicial proceeding, witnesses are examined twice: the examination and cross-examination phases. The extract above demonstrates a cross-examination phase, that is, the defence lawyer's examination, yet, the state counsel questioned the witness in line 23. Annoyed, the defence lawyer uses a behabitive illocutionary act in lines 27 and 28, where he reported this misconduct to the judge.

In case 21, the behabitive illocutionary act was not use by a lawyer but by a judge.

65. AC: Mais tu viens de dire que tu étais chez toi quand tu as entendu les
66. cris. Donc tu étais au champs et chez toi en même temps. <*But you have just said that you were in your house when you heard shouts. So you were at your place and in the farm at the same time*>
67. J: Quelle est la question? <*What is the questions*>
68. AC: Où étais-tu? <*Where were you?*>

In lines 65 and 66, the accused was in the posture of a lawyer, but he did not properly formulate his questions. The judge reprimanded him in line 67 without considering his lack of judicial knowledge. Actually, the accused represented himself because he did not have the financial means to pay for the services of a lawyer.

Another accused who received the behabitive illocutionary act of a judge was the accused of case 29 of the observation guide.

8. GR: Mr., levez la main droite et répétez après moi: « Je jure de dire la
9. vérité » <*Sir, raise your right hand and repeat after me: "I swear to tell the truth"*>
10. AC: « Je dis de dire la vérité » <*"I say to tell the truth"*>
11. J: C'est: « je jure de dire la vérité » <*It is: "I swear to tell the truth*>
12. AC: Je jouir de dire la vérité <*i swar to tell the truth*>
13. GR: Rien que la vérité <*Only the truth*>
14. AC: Rien que la vérité <*Only the truth*>

The accused was 'unable' to repeat the clerk's words. Instead of saying « Je jure de dire la vérité », he rather said « Je dis de dire la vérité ». The judge corrected the accused in line 11, but even after the judge's correction, the accused did not succeed to repeat the said sentence. He used the word 'jouir' (bubble) instead of 'jure' (swear). Indeed, the accused linguistic background (first language) did not provide him with the linguistic tools to properly repeat the French sentences. Once more, the background knowledge of a litigant was not taking into consideration by a legal authority.

- Exercitive acts

In exercitives acts, speakers also condemn, but here the speaker is an authority exercising his power or influence. It is not uncommon to see court participants, both legal professionals and litigants, misbehaving during trials. The judge role is to bring order in court by condemning any misconduct. Exercitives illocutionary acts are more harmful to litigants than to legal professionals. In fact, exercitive speech acts often penalise litigants during the deliberation.

In case 3, the judge directed his exercitive act to the accused because he used a language different from the language of the court.

25. AC: I have never seen it!
26. SC: But this is your signature /showing the statement to the AC/
27. AC: 'je n'ai jamais dit ça, moi je n'ai jamais dit ça!' <*I have never said that, me I have never said that!*>
28. J: Speak in Pidgin!

In the Court of First Instance of Buea, trials are conducted in English and eventually in Pidgin English, but the accused frequently used French. The language switching of the accused annoyed the judge who ordered the accused to use Pidgin English. Sadly, the judge did not consider the linguistics competence of the accused. A francophone was compelled to defend himself in Pidgin English, a language he does not master.

In case 21, the plaintiff received the exercitive act of the judge because of his misconduct. In the extract below, the plaintiff corrected the lawyer's question in line 15. This annoyed the judge who ordered him to answer the question of the lawyer. Once again, I note the case of a legal authority who is not receptive to the shortfalls of a lay-litigant.

9. AD: Vous avez des attestations de succession? <*do you have an attestation of succession?*>
10. PL: Ce n'est pas ce type de questions que vous devez me poser. <*This is not the type of question that you should ask me*>
11. J: Répondez à la question. <*Answer the question*!>

- Receptive acts

Exceedingly, Cameroon legal professional's illocutionary speech acts often considered the litigants' background knowledge (IS theory). I noted many cases were legal authorities addresses litigants in their preferred languages to break down language barriers. Other legal authorities chose to use simpler words to allow the lay-litigants to understand the discussion. I chose to call this form of illocutionary act receptive illocutionary acts. I define receptive illocutionary acts as speeches that consider the background knowledge and abilities of hearers. Thus, in receptive acts, the speaker adopts an attitude of sympathy to his hearer. Two court extracts demonstrate instances of receptive illocutionary acts observed in Cameroon courtrooms.

Case 3 (three) of our observation guide:

6. J: /presents the accusation and the corresponding condemnation in English/
7. AC: (.)
8. J: you don understand weti I just tok? < *did you understand what I just said?*>
9. AC: No sir.
10. J: You hear but you no understand. All the big book mean say (…) < *you heard but you didn't understand. In fact, this is what I said …*>

Case 11 (eleven) of the observation guide:

1. J: The accused has been found guilty of phone stealing and of moving
2. without a national ID meanwhile, he is 20 years old.
3. CK: Court don find you guilty, beg mek court no ova punish you. <*You have been found guilty, ask that your sentence be reduced*>
4. AC: I beg mek court no ova punish me /he kneels down/ < *I ask the court to reduce my sentence*>
5. J: Stand up. Sentence count 1: convict shall pay a fine of 30000frs, count
6. 2: convict shall pay to the plaintiff an amount of 70000frs and to the
7. government 44000frs.
8. CK: /He repeat the sentence in Pidgin English/

In case 3, the judge understood that the accused's silence was due to the fact that he did not understand the English language. The judge, therefore, explained the court's verdict in a language the accused knew better, Pidgin English. In case 11, the clerk made the same observation; the accused did not understand the English language. And like the judge in the previous case, the clerk explained the court's verdict in a language the accused understood better. It is important to note that the actions of the judge and the clerk do not comply with section 183 of the Criminal Procedure Code of Cameroon, which stipulate that 'the registrar, witnesses and the parties shall not perform the functions of an interpreter'. But the linguistic inequality of the court (the non-inclusive language policy and the absence of the interpreters) pushed the legal authorities to sympathies to the language problems of the lay-litigants. In sum, though some legal authorities' illocutionary acts did not consider the background knowledge of litigants. Others, on the other hand, were more sympathetic.

Conclusion

This chapter presented the data collected in the Courts of First Instance of Bafoussam, Buea, Douala, Yaoundé and Ngaoundéré. I analysed and discussed the data using the SAT and the IS principles of knowledge of institutional codes of conducts. The analysis demonstrated that lay-litigants violated two Felicity conditions (Conventionality and Actuality conditions). However, I noted that these violations were not dilatory tactics, but rather expressions of linguistic difficulties and/or barrier. Indeed, lay-litigants violated the Conventionality condition when answering legal professional questions in their first languages (national languages) and the Actuality condition when misinterpreting words or sentences. To reprimand lay-litigants violation of the Felicity conditions, legal authorities used exercitives, verdictives, and behabitives acts. However, I observed another form of illocutionary acts used by Cameroon legal professionals, the receptive illocutionary act. Therefore, the analysis of Cameroon courtroom discourse allowed me to add a sixth illocutionary category to the five already developed by Austin (1962) and Searle (1969). Literature has rarely highlighted the receptive attitude of legal professionals during courtroom discourse. For instance, Bhatia (2017) and Chaemsaithong (2012) demonstrated that legal stakeholders never tried to make their words to ordinary citizens understandable. Legal texts are written in a highly nominal style rather than verbal style. He and Feng's (2016) analysis of Chinese courtroom discourse indicated that legal professionals use 'channeling discourse' to divert the litigants to legal or extra-legal institutions. And in this chapter, I showed that receptive illocutionary acts are used in cases of flagrant language barrier. In other words, legal professional utter receptive illocutionary act to break the language barrier that prevents the litigant from answering the examiner questions. The analysis of Cameroon courtroom discourse allowed me to demonstrate how legal professionals practice law in court, but to determine how they developed the skills and constructed their attitude towards the language problems of the legal system, I consulted (interview) them.

References

Aspers, P., & Corte, U. (2019). What is qualitative in qualitative research. *Qualitative Sociology, 42*, 139–160. https://doi.org/10.1007/s11133-019-9413-7

Austin, J. L. (1962). *How to do things with words*. Oxford University Press.

Bernard, R. H. (2006). *Research methods in anthropology: Qualitative and quantitative approaches* (4th ed.). AltaMira Press.

Bhatia, V. K. (2017). Interpreting law in socio-pragmatic space. *Semiotica, 2017*(216), 109–130.

Bogdan, R. C. (1972). *Participant observation in organized settings*. Syracuse University Press.

Chaemsaithong, K. (2012). Performing self on the witness stand: Stance and relational work in expert witness testimony. *Discourse & Society, 23*(5), 465–486.

Criminal Procedure Code of the Republic of Cameroon. (2005a). Art. 3(2).

Criminal Procedure Code of the Republic of Cameroon. (2005b). Art. 170(2).

Denzin, N. K., & Lincoln, Y. S. (2005). Introduction. The discipline and practice of qualitative research. In N. K. Denzin & Y. S. Lincoln (Eds.), *The Sage handbook of qualitative research* (pp. 1–32). SAGE Publications.

Dornyei, Z. (2007). *Research methods in applied linguistics: Quantitative, qualitative and mixed methodologies*. Oxford University Press.

Eberhard, D. M., Simons, G. F., & Fennig, C. D. (Eds.). (2019). *Ethnologue: Languages of the world* (22nd ed.). SIL International. Retrieved from http://www.ethnologue.com

Eggins, S., & Slade, D. (1997). *Analysing casual conversation*. Cassell.

English, F. (2010). Non-native speakers in detention: Assessing non-native speaking detainees' English language proficiency. In M. Coulthard & A. Johnson (Eds.), *The Routledge handbook of forensic linguistics* (pp. 423–440). Routledge.

Etsuko, O. (2006). Austin's speech act theory and the speech situation. *Esercizi Filosofici, 1*, 1–14.

Goodwin, J., & Horowitz, R. (2002). Introduction. The methodological strengths and dilemmas of qualitative sociology. *Qualitative Sociology, 25*(1), 33–47.

Gumperz, J. (2001). Interactional sociolinguistics: A personal perspective. In D. Schiffrin, D. Tannen, & E. Hamilton (Eds.), *The handbook of discourse analysis* (pp. 220–250). Blackwell.

He, X., & Feng, Y. (2016). Mismatched discourses in the petition of Chinese courts. *Law & Social Inquiry, 41*(1), 212–241.

Jürgen, J. (2011). Interaction sociolinguistics and discourse analysis. In J. P. Gee & M. Handford (Eds.), *The Routledge handbook of discourse analysis* (pp. 135–146). Routledge.

Kumar, R. (2011). *Research methodology: A step by step guide for beginners* (3rd ed.). Sage.

McCarthy, M., Matthiessen, C., & Slade, D. (2010). Discourse analysis. In N. Schmitt (Ed.), *An introduction to applied linguistics* (pp. 53–70). Hodder Education.

Searle, J. (1969). *Speech acts: An essay in the philosophy of language*. Cambridge University Press.

Searle, J. (1975). Indirect speech acts. In C. Peter & J. L. Morgan (Eds.), *Syntax and semantics* (pp. 59–82). Academic Press.

Virbel, J. (2015). Speech act theory and instructional texts. In K. Chemla & J. Virbel (Eds.), *Textual acts and the history of science* (pp. 49–58). Springer.

Walliman, N. (2011). *Research methods: The basics*. Routledge.

CHAPTER 5

Consultation with Legal Professionals

Introduction

The legal profession is a vocation, and legal professionals study, develop, and apply the law. Usually, there is a requirement for someone choosing a career in law to first obtain a law degree or some other form of legal education. Chapter 4 demonstrated how Cameroon legal professionals apply the law in courtrooms. Chapter 5 aims to define what makes up the training of legal professionals in Cameroon. It is clear that to be a legal professional you need to know the law, but the content of this work already demonstrated that within the law we have language. All those involved in legal matters need to speak and listen to a language. Therefore, in courtrooms, legal professionals should consider both the legal and language issues of litigants.

With the aid of semi-structured interview guides, I interviewed Cameroon Bench Magistrates (judges), magistrates (state counsels), lawyers, and interpreters to know how they were equipped and prepared to face the legal language-related problems of the nation. In other words, I seek to explain legal professionals' use of the behabitives, exercitives, verdictives, and receptive illocutionary speech acts in courtrooms.

E. M. K. Dissake, *Language and Legal Proceedings*,
https://doi.org/10.1007/978-3-030-76349-7_5

Semi-structured Interviews

Interviews are qualitative methods of data collection through which researchers ask to a sample population sets of questions designed to obtain particular information regarding a research problem and question. Monette et al. (1986) argued that 'an interview involves an interviewer reading questions to respondents and recording their answers' (p. 156). And Burns (1997) added that 'an interview is a verbal interchange [...] in which an interviewer tries to elicit information [...]' (p. 329). Interviews are classified into different categories, unstructured, structured, and semi-structured interviews.

A researcher selection of an interview category depends on the level of flexibility of his/her topic of research. The category chosen in the present research is found in between the unstructured and the structured interview, that is, the semi-structured interview. There is less flexibility in a semi-structured interview, the interviewer directs the interview more closely, and some of the questions are predetermined. It can be difficult to differentiate an unstructured interview from a semi-structured interview. However, the general agreement is that unstructured interviews are mostly controlled by the interviewee meanwhile semi-structured interviews have predefined areas of discussions prepared in advance by the researcher (interviewer). Moreover, unlike unstructured interviews, semi-structured as well as structured interviews possess interview schedules or guides. An interview guide is a list of open and closed-ended questions prepared in advance by the interviewer and later on asked to the interviewee during the interviewing session. It is important to note that interview guides are considered to be research instruments while interviewing is a method of data collection. Developing and processing an interview involves various stages among which drafting, piloting, sampling, administrating, and analysing.

In this research, I made use of two interview guides. The first guide was administered to legal authorities and translated in both official languages (English and French). The French version was administered in Civil law districts (Yaoundé, Douala, Bafoussam, and Ngaoundéré), and the English version was administered in a Common law district (Buea). The legal authorities' interview guide was drafted and piloted in Buea by the author. And as its name shows, the selected interviewees were legal authorities working in Cameroon courtrooms, that is Bench Magistrates, state counsels, and lawyers. The interviews were conducted and analysed by the author. The legal authority interview guide is structured as such: (1) opening statement, (2) training, (3) practice, (4) attitudinal scale, and (5) additional information (suggestions). And the questions move from general inquiries like *Do you know the literacy level of Cameroonian? Or can you estimate it?* to specific questioning like *What is your working language?*

The second interview guide was in the French language and was administered to the interpreter of the Ngaoundéré Court of First Instance. This interview guide was drafted and piloted in Ngaoundéré. The guide was only in the French language because it was administered in a Civil law district, Ngaoundéré, a francophone city. This interview guide consisted of opening remarks and nine questions, all related to the linguistics competence of the interpreter. And it was administered to a single interpreter because Cameroon courts rarely call for the assistance of interpreters. As demonstrated in Chap. 4, many lay-litigants do not enjoy the assistance of interpreters during court discourse.

The two interview guides had head notes where the following information was noted: location, date of interview, name of the interviewer, number assigned to the interviewee, the start time and end time, and an introductory statement. In the introductory statement, I introduced myself, stated the structure and the objective of the interview, assured the respondent of the confidentiality of his/her response, and asked permission to audiotape the discussion. At the end of each interview sessions, I summarised the respondents' answers for the sake of accuracy. I interviewed a total of 15 legal practitioners among which were 5 Bench Magistrates (judges), 4 state counsels, 5 lawyers, and 1 interpreter, as demonstrated in the chart below (Fig. 5.1):

Lay-litigants were not interviewed first because I did not have access to them. Second, the judicial system of Cameroon does not allow external parties to discuss with litigants throughout the judicial proceedings. However, I took note of the language problems encountered by the lay-litigants during the court discourse. Indeed, the absence of answers, the non-coherent and/or inappropriate answers, and the grammatical mistakes of the litigants provided me with enough information concerning their linguistic profiles. Also, the legal practitioners' interviews enabled me to determine if the language problems faced by lay-litigants were understood by the court authorities.

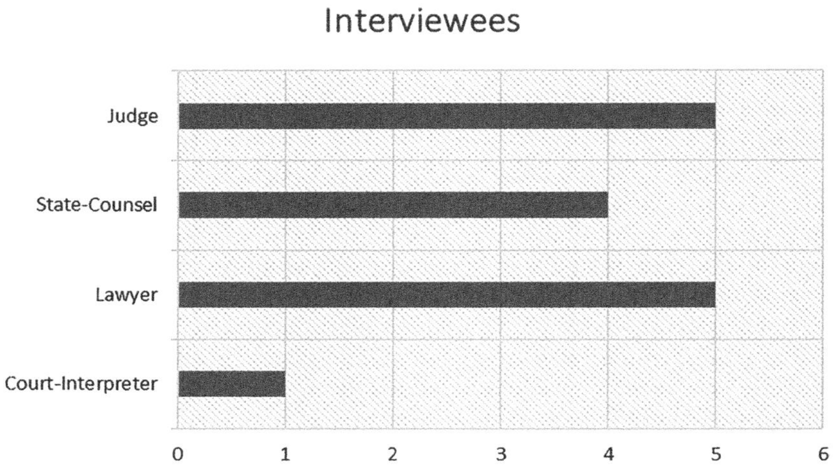

Fig. 5.1 Interviewees

Legal Authority's Interview

To conduct the interviews, I first had to sample the interviewees. The role of sampling in qualitative research is to find individuals who will provide rich insights on the topic of discussion and as such help in solving the research problem and answer the research question. I purposively selected the legal practitioners who had a well-built experience in judicial proceedings and who could help me to explain the attitude of legal professionals towards the linguistic limitations of lay-litigants. To lay hands on this type of respondents, I used non-probability sampling strategies like snowball sampling, opportunity sampling, judgemental/purposive sampling, and expert sampling. However, before starting this strategy I was already in contact with some lawyers with whom I was able to pilot the interview guide. But I needed more respondents, and most importantly I needed to interview legal professionals of all the five Courts of First Instance where I collected the discourse. It was difficult to meet legal practitioners such as judges and ask them a bit of their time for an interview. It's easy to run into a lawyer in a law firm, but it's hard to run into a magistrate and ask for a little of his time. Nevertheless, I was able to accost some magistrate at the end of trials. All the interviews were conducted in interviewees' offices. Below, I discussed the four sections of the legal authority interview guide (introduction, training period, working period, and suggestions).

- Section 1: Introduction

Since the research topic was FL and this is a research area little known in Cameroon, it was necessary to initiate a discussion on this subject. At the start of each interview, I first tried to find out if the interviewee was familiar with this research topic or at least if he knew what it was about. Without surprise none of the legal professionals interviewed had ever heard about Forensic Linguistics, none could relate this field of study to law, and none could even link language to law. I was even amused to hear a lawyer saying that 'FL has to do with extraordinary and mystical phenomenon'. This state of affairs therefore explains why linguists are never called to court as expert witness. Before starting the next steps of the interviews, I defined and described the field of Forensic Linguistics to the interviewees. It was necessary to show the link that exists between language and law, and to explain that linguistics could provide solutions to the language problems that we observed in law.

- Section 2: Training period

Legal professionals receive training to instil them the knowledge of the law, prepare them to say the law and face problems related to law. Given the language problems observed during debates and the attitude of lawmakers to these problems, it was important to know how their training prepared them to face this type of problem. In Cameroon, magistrates (state counsels and judges) are trained in ENAM 'L'École nationale d'administration et de la magistrature' (National School of Administration and Magistracy), and lawyers are trained in various law schools, among which, The Faculty of Legal and Political Sciences of the University of Yaoundé II. The interviewed magistrates declared that during their training at ENAM, the trainers never alluded to the language problems that could encounter the litigants during courtroom discourse. The only linguistics training they received was bilingualism training. Because the law operates in the two official languages (English and French), magistrates are trained to speak and to understand both languages. Yet, apart from English and French, Cameroon counts more than 250 national languages. Therefore, the national languages of Cameroon are extirpated from the roots of the judicial system (legal schools). But, some magistrate argued that the judicial system of Cameroon recognises the cultural diversity of the nation, this is why during the training in ENAM, they had a course called, 'Multiculturalism'. The purpose of the course was to train the magistrates to adapt the law of the nation to the cultural diversity of their region of assignment. For instance, in the far north of the country, culture approves forced marriages and marriages of underage girls. When confronted with this type of case, the magistrate should not condemn anyone if the two families agree. Thus, the law of Cameroon adapts to the culture but do not adapt to the languages of the cultures.

Lawyers training is different from that of magistrates. For instance, they are not trained to use both official languages and to adapt the law to the culture of the citizens. Their training focuses on their fight for the respect of their client's rights. Lawyers admitted that they were taught to use the law to defend their clients, but their trainers never explained that the negligence of their client's mother tongues could be detrimental. It is by practising law that they have all been able to observe that many litigants faced linguistic difficulties during the trials. Both magistrates and lawyers admitted that although English and French are the official languages of Cameroon, many litigants are unable to use those languages, especially in the legal context. A state counsel remembered the case of a man accused of theft who pleaded guilty. The plaintiff of the case requested ten million, but the accused argued that he only stole six million, yet he pleaded guilty. Thus, some litigants could not define basic terms like guilty or not guilty. Such elements demonstrate the degree of linguistics barriers in Cameroon courtrooms.

- Section 3: Working period

After striving to understand the training system of Cameroon legal professionals, I required to know if they faced legal language-related problems after taking up their duties. All legal authorities admitted having been confronted to legal language-related problems during trials. Lawyers, state counsels, and judges declared that they are constantly chatting with litigants who cannot express themselves in the language of the court. On the one hand, we have francophones involved in judicial issues in Common law districts and on the other hand Anglophones involved in judicial issues in Civil law districts. Yet, the problem is not limited to English and/or French. Some litigants are not literate in either French or English but are rather proficient in one or more Cameroon national languages. A lawyer recalled the case of an accused who spoke only his mother tongue but was tried in English in the Buea Court of First Instance.

All interviewees witnessed at list one case where a litigant first language was not the language of the court. Therefore, I requested to know what solution they preconise for such problems. Some of them informed me of specific methods. Legal professionals exercising in the Common law districts use Pidgin English to communicate with lay-litigants. Pidgin English is a language of wider communication; it is a language that even the least literate in the English-speaking region masters well. However, data analysis in Chap. 4 demonstrates that not all litigants tried in Common law districts are native of the regions. Some litigants who were francophones tried in English-speaking courts and compelled to defend themselves in Pidgin English, a language they do not master. Other litigants were anglophones who could only communicate in their mother tongues, Cameroon national languages. Thus, the use of Pidgin English in an English-speaking courtroom is not always the best linguistic solution to the language problems of lay-litigants.

In Civil law districts, legal professionals often choose to call interpreters when the situation is such that they cannot do otherwise. Though the presence of interpreters in case of linguistics barrier is mandatory, those interpreters are rarely present in courtrooms. As a matter of fact, many Magistrates admitted that they rarely requested the services of interpreters when confronted to English-speaking litigants because they prefer to rely on their knowledge of English acquired at ENAM. When the anglophone litigants realise that they are not well understood, they make the effort to express themselves in French. Thus, it's the litigants who adapt to the language of the court and not the court that adapts to the language of the litigants.

Even though interpreter's presence in case of language problems are mandatory, it is difficult to lay hands on good court interpreters in Cameroon. Many court interpreters are not trained, and some legal authorities declared that 'their presence in court is more harmful than beneficial'. In Cameroon, court interpreters are either litigants' relatives or ad-hoc interpreters selected in the audience. Courts rarely used trained interpreters because they are too costly. Actually, the law recommended the use of interpreters in courts without providing funds to pay their services. Most often, interpreters' services are paid by individuals (litigants, litigants relatives, or courts presidents), though it is the state responsibility. However, I noted that interpreters are frequently assigned to rural and/or semi-urban courts, for instance, the Courts of First Instance of Bafoussam and Ngaoundéré. This may be because the population literacy rate is lower in those districts.

The lawyers made me know that when the presence of an interpreter is essential for the hearings, the search for a good interpreter can last for months and even for years. Litigants who are not willing to wait, feel obligated to look for an interpreter by themselves. Most often, those interpreters are untrained relatives. A judge recalled the case of an aged woman who understood only Bulu.[1] The court searched for an interpreter for various months to no avail. Finally, the woman called her grandson, but the grandson's interpretation was suboptimal. The services of an untrained interpreter can have devastating effects on the overall hearings and verdict.

- Section 4: Interviewees' suggestions

After noting the lack of interest that the Cameroon legal system has in the national languages and the linguistic difficulties encountered by litigants, I requested legal professionals to advance solutions to the dilemmas. While few proposed the introduction of national languages in the legal system, many rejected this possibility on the premises that Cameroon has too many national languages (more than 250 languages). Indeed, those against the introduction of national languages in the legal system dwelled on the problem of number. They argued that the system could hardly manage such a number of languages. A state counsel even alluded that the introduction of national languages will pose a problem of translation and interpretation. Since Cameroon national languages are not developed, it will be difficult to render a legal text in those languages. Moreover, legal jargon is a specialised language. Because it is difficult to translate a legal text from a developed language to another developed language (the case of English and French in Canada) it will be more difficult to translate from a developed language to a less developed one. However, through the development of key legal terms in Tunen (a language spoken in the Littoral and Central Regions of Cameroon), Atindogbé and Dissake (2019) refuted the fallacy that African languages could not express abstract

[1] Bulu is a Bantu language patterning to the Ewondo-Fang (A.74) group. Bulu is used as LWC throughout the South Region and also (less so) in the East Region of Cameroon (Eberhard et al., 2019).

realities. Another point raised to go against the introduction of national languages in the legal system is that those languages are already used in customary courts. Yet, the Customary court's ordinance cap 142 of 1948 defines customary law as 'the native law and custom prevailing in the area of the jurisdiction of the court so far as it is not repugnant to natural justice, equity and good conscience, nor incompatible either directly or by natural implication with the written law for the time being in force'. Therefore, statutory law has control over customary laws, and not all cases are brought to the customary systems. So, the use of national languages in customary courts should not exclude the introduction of those languages in statutory courts.

Those for the introduction of the national languages proposed a solution relative to its high number. They proposed a selection process based on the principle of predominance, in other words, they suggested that national languages with the highest number of native speakers should be introduced in the legal system. This suggestion follows the postulate of 'the majority win', yet, the trend is on the protection of minorities. Indeed, no one should feel excluded, the best language policy of a multilingual nation is an inclusive policy. Another suggestion was the introduction of national languages in law schools. Some interviewees explained that national languages could be used in law schools like ENAM so magistrates could have the right to address litigants in their mother tongues.

Even though opinions differ regarding the initiation of national languages in Cameroon courtrooms, all the interviewees agreed on three points, the provision of legal assistance, the training of courtroom interpreters, and the introduction of language experts.

I realised that more than 70% of litigants were prosecuted in the absence of lawyers because many litigants cannot afford lawyers services. Section 417 of the Criminal Procedure Code states that;

> Section 417:
>
> (1) The Presiding Judge shall ascertain whether the accused bas briefed counsel for his defense
>
> (2) Where the accused is being prosecuted for a felony punishable with death or loss of liberty for life and he has no counsel, the Presiding Judge shall of his own motion assign one to him.
>
> (3) The Presiding Judge may of his own motion assign only counsel accused person where their interest do not conflict. (Criminal Procedure Code of the Republic of Cameroon, 2005)

The legal system of Cameroon provides lawyers only to accused persons prosecuted for a felony punishable by death or loss of liberty for life. Therefore, lay-litigants who can't afford the services of a lawyer and who are deprived of the assistance of an interpreter, are heard and tried in a language they do not master.

Other interviewees advocated for the effective training of court interpreters. They argued that poor interpretation creates great language problems during judicial proceedings. For instance, in case 23 of our observation guide, an interpreter whispered his translation in the judge ears. It is therefore evident that the interpreter does not know that the court's code of conduct demand that all parties should hear the translation of the interpreter in order to call the judge's attention in the case of a miscarriage. Nevertheless, one interviewee argued that poor interpretation wouldn't be a problem if judges were attentive. For him, what happened in case 23 could have been cleared up if the judge had brought back the interpreter to order. It was up to the judge to tell the interpreter to speak aloud to allow the audience to listen to him. In other words, judges should pay more attention to the actions of interpreters. However, the interpreters used in the courts should receive adequate training.

Another suggestion was the introduction of language experts in courts. Despite that Cameroon legal professionals do not have a good knowledge of the field of linguistic or even Forensic Linguistic studies, many proposed that language issues should be handled by linguists. Linguistic expertise must be introduced in courtrooms in order to help those lay-litigants who at times are unfairly treated because of linguistic barriers. Because English and French are taught in schools, used in offices, spoken on radios and televisions, the tendency is to believe that the linguistic mistakes of litigants are dilatory tactics. For many, all Cameroonians are literate in either English or French. But, Chap. 4 demonstrated that lay-litigants encounter real linguistic problems during courtroom discourse, and those problems could be analysed and resolved by language experts (expert witness) (Table 5.1).

Court Interpreter Interview

The importance of interpreters in trials is fully recognised. However, interpreters' elections and working methods vary from one legal system to another. For instance, in Cameroon, Section 183 of the Criminal Procedure Code outline why and how court interpreters are elected.

Table 5.1 Interview summary

No	*Theme*	*Respond*
1	Forensic Linguistics (FL)	Interviewees had ever heard of FL.
2	Language training	Interviewees were not trained to face the language problems of the legal system of Cameroon.
3	Legal language problems	All the interviewees have already witness cases were litigants could not communicate in the court language.
4	Court interpreters	All the interviewees noted the incompetence of interpreters.
5	Suggestion	Although opinions differ regarding the initiation of national languages in Cameroon courtrooms, all the interviewees agreed on three points, the provision of legal assistance, the training of courtroom interpreters, and the introduction of language experts.

(a) Where a witness does not speak one of the official languages which the registrar and Examining Magistrate understand; the latter shall call on the services of an interpreter.

(b) The interpreter shall not be less than twenty-one (21) years of age.

(c) The registrar, witnesses and the parties shall not perform the functions of an interpreter.

(d) The interpreter shall take oath to give a true interpretation of the statement of any person who speaks in different language or dialect. The facts of his having taken oath shall be mentioned in the record of the proceedings. (Criminal Procedure Code of the Republic of Cameroon, 2005)

The Criminal Procedure Code of Cameroon advocate for the presence of an interpreter in judicial cases involving lay-litigants. Yet, those interpreters are rarely present in courtrooms. According to legal professionals, the absence of interpreters is due to the fact that the government did not assign a budget to pay for their services, therefore, cannot afford their services. Nonetheless, rural and semi-urban districts established interpreters who work regularly in courtrooms. The reason is that the literacy level of the adult population of those districts is low, many have never been to schools. My observation and the interviews established that the services rendered by those established interpreters are never satisfactory. I interviewed the court interpreter of the legal district of Ngaoundéré to understand why established court interpreters' works are unsatisfactory. During the interview, I seek to know why the choice was carried on him, in which school he was trained and which method of translation he followed. The interpreter interview guide was divided into two sections, introduction and language use.

- Section 1: Introduction

The interpreter of the Ngaoundéré Court of First Instance is a man of 67 years. At the start of the interview, I required to know if he had received any interpretation training. The interviewee admitted that he has never gone through a training school. He used to be a primary school teacher, but when his brother was appointed state counsel for the Ngaoundéré Court of First Instance, his brother regularly calls him to perform some tasks. Because he spoke several languages of the region, he was elected court interpreter of the Ngaoundéré Court of First Instance in 2004. Therefore, to the question, do Cameroon court interpreters passed through training school? The answer is No. Court interpreters are mere bilinguals or multilinguals. They are selected by affinity, as is the case of the interpreter of the Court of First Instance of Ngaoundéré. He was elected thanks to his kinship with state counsel. This absence of training, therefore, explains why Cameroon court Interpreters' performance is not up to standard.

- Section 2: Language use

The town of Ngaoundéré is the regional capital of the Adamawa region of Cameroon. Therefore, the national languages spoken in Ngaoundéré fall within the Adamawa language group. The Adamawa languages are a putative family of 80–90 languages scattered across the Adamawa Plateau in central Africa, Nigeria, Cameroon, Central African Republic, and Chad, spoken altogether by only one and a half million people (Greenberg, 1963).

Of the 30 languages spoken in the region, the interviewer claims to speak at least 18, among which are Fulfulde, Mandara, and sign language. But when asked if he could maintain a long discussion with natives of those 18 languages, he admits only mastering 5 of those 18 languages. Though he only masters 5 languages, he interprets in 18 languages. He makes abundant use of modalities (signs and gestures) to give more meanings to his words when he interprets in languages he does not master.

However, he recognised not been always sure of what to say in those circumstances.

Since I was surprised to hear that he also interpreted in sign language, I tried to know the name of the sign language and how he learned it. Three sign languages are used in Cameroon: the French sign language, the American sign language, and the Cameroon sign language. The French sign language is taught in the French-speaking regions, the American sign language is taught in the English-speaking regions, and the Cameroon sign language is a new sign language developed to reflect the realities of Cameroon; it is still very little used in the country (Dissake & Atindogbé, 2019). The interviewee uses neither of those sign languages. He was not even aware that there exist different sign languages. What he called sign language are mere body movements he developed in his childhood to communicate with his hearing-impaired neighbours.

Conclusion

Cameroon legal professionals demonstrated that they neither understand nor measure the legal language-related problems of courtrooms. Indeed, they are not trained to do so. Magistrates and lawyers training schools do not introduce their trainees to the language issues of the law. Languages are completely dissociated from the law. The judicial system imposes English and French on all litigants without considering their first or preferred languages. The exercitives and verdictives illocutionary speech acts of legal professionals are a consequence of the exclusion of linguistic instruments in the judiciary.

Though the law proposes interpreter's assistance in trials involving lay-litigants, interpreters are rarely present in courtrooms. Two main reasons account for this, the lack of finance and the scarceness of skilled interpreters. Anglophone legal districts tried to solve the problem by using Pidgin English (a language of wider communication) in courts. But the data analysis demonstrated that only Pidgin English cannot solve the language problems of courtrooms. As for rural and semi-urban areas like Ngaoundéré, they elect multilinguals as court interpreters to assist lay-litigants. However, the interviews demonstrated that those elected interpreters are not trained to perform the function.

To solve the legal language-related problems of Cameroon courtrooms, legal professionals suggested the training of court interpreters and the assistance of linguistic experts. Linguists (expert witness) should be called upon when legal professionals observe language issues in judicial proceedings.

References

Atindogbé, G. G., & Dissake, K. M. E. (2019). Forensic linguistics as a tool for the development of Cameroon national languages. *African Study Monographs, 40*(1), 23–44. https://doi.org/10.14989/243208

Burns, R. B. (1997). *An introduction to research method* (2nd ed.). Longman.

Criminal Procedure Code of the Republic of Cameroon. (2005). Art. 417(1–3).

Dissake, K. M. E., & Atindogbé, G. G. (2019). *Deaf education and language-based curriculum: The case of the Buea School for the Deaf.* OAsis, COL's Open Access Repository. http://hdl.handle.net/11599/3431

Eberhard, D. M., Simons, G. F., & Fennig, C. D. (Eds.). (2019). *Ethnologue: Languages of the world* (22nd ed.). SIL International. Retrieved from http://www.ethnologue.com

Greenberg, J. H. (1963). *The languages of Africa.* Indiana University Press.

Monette, D. R., Thomas, J. S., & Cornell, R. D. (1986). *Applied social research to human services.* Holt, Rinehart, and Winston.

CHAPTER 6

Concluding Remarks

To carry out the analysis of Cameroon courtroom discourse, I first described the legal and language policy of Cameroon. Chapter 2 of this book demonstrated that the bilingual and bijural policies of Cameroon are a vestige of colonialism. Both policies promote bilingualism. English and French are the exclusive languages of the law though Cameroon counts more than 250 national languages. The exclusive language policy of the law disadvantages lay-litigants. To adequately analyse the legal language problems of Cameroon, I first reviewed the methods used by other scholars in other legal settings (America, Britain, Australia, China, and South Africa). Thus, Chap. 3 reviewed literature on FL studies. The description of different FL studies enriched my analysis of the discourse collected in Cameroon Courts of First Instance. I analysed Cameroon courtroom discourse with the overall theory of Discourse Analysis in Chap. 4. The analysis established that Cameroon legal professionals use unconventional illocutionary acts, and lay-litigants violate speech Felicity conditions because they are not literate in the court languages. Chapter 5 explained the attitude (the illocutionary acts) of the legal professionals through the analysis of the semi-structured interview administered on them. The interviews revealed that legal professionals were not prepared to face the language-related problems of Cameroon courtrooms, and court interpreters are not trained interpreters. This last chapter (Chap. 6) summarises and concludes the study.

E. M. K. Dissake, *Language and Legal Proceedings*,
https://doi.org/10.1007/978-3-030-76349-7_6

The analysis of Cameroon courtroom discourse outlined both general and specific legal language-related problems. First, the general problems are those main elements that hinder communication in courtrooms. I identified three of them, the language policy of the law, the fragmented training of legal professionals, and the absence of skilled interpreters.

The Language Policy of the Law

As specified in Article 31, section 3 of the Cameroon Constitution, all judicial proceedings are conducted in English and French (official languages). In Common law districts (English-speaking regions), the law is said in English. And in Civil law districts (French-speaking regions), legal proceedings are conducted in French. Indeed, English and French were used in 95% of the court discourse collected and presented in Chap. 3, and Pidgin English was used in the remaining 5%. However, 100% of the discourse involved lay-litigants, people facing difficulty communicating in English and/or French. Therefore, Essono's (2001) analysis which demonstrated that 40% of the adult population are illiterate in the official languages is verified in courtrooms.

In the light of my analysis, I argue that 90% of litigants prosecuted in Cameroon Courts of First Instance are not proficient in English and/or French. Thus, English and French constitute a major language problem in courtrooms. The state should render the language policy more inclusive, that is, introduce national languages in the legal setting. In Chap. 4, legal professionals suggested ways through which national languages could be introduced in courtrooms.

The Fragmented Training of Legal Professionals

In the interviews, legal professionals admitted that they were not familiarised with the language issues of the law during their training. Hence, the following elements were unknown to them:

(a) English and French constitute a language barrier to many litigants.
(b) The testimonies of litigants can be more precise and unambiguous if they are said in national languages.
(c) The presence of an untrained interpreter in the court constitutes a language problem for the hearing.

Schools of law focalise on the content of the law only, its mode of transmission (languages) and its related problems are not discussed. Therefore, legal professionals discover Cameroon legal language-related problems in the field. And the later independently remedy to the problems through proceedings that are not always to the advantage of litigants. For instance, some legal professionals promote the use of the language of wider communication (e.g. Pidgin English) and the presence of untrained interpreters in courts.

To complete the training of legal professionals, that is, to prepare the later to face legal language-related problems, I suggest the introduction of language courses in law schools. Law schools should open the debate of language barriers in courts. Though legal professionals are not linguists, they however need to understand the language issues of the law. This knowledge will enable them to understand (1) the language problems that lay-litigants encounter, (2) the negative effects of a poor legal interpretation, (3) and the role of a language expert in legal matters.

The Absence of Skilled Interpreters

Section 183 of the Cameroon Criminal Procedure Code advocates for the presence of interpreters in trials involving lay-litigants. Yet, the legal system does not provide the means to implement this law. Interpreters are rarely present in courtrooms, and when they are present, their interpretation is never effective. Indeed, interpreters present in Cameroon courtrooms are rarely trained. Most often, they are litigants' relatives or bilinguals selected on the spot. Even in legal departments where interpreters are elected, the interpretation skills of the latter are not a basic prerequisite. For instance, the elected court interpreter of Ngaoundéré is not a trained interpreter (he is a school's teacher), he pretends to be proficient in 18 languages, but he masters only 5 languages. The ineffective interpretation of court interpreters often affects hearings. For example, the elected interpreter of the Court of First Instance of Bafoussam whispered his translation in the ears of the judge. Hence, the interpretation was not verified by every court member.

In a multilingual nation like Cameroon, the training of court interpreters should be at the top of the priorities of the judicial body. Legal interpretation is among the most technical type of interpretation (Hale, 2010). A legal interpreter should not only be bilingual. In other words, legal interpreters should not only master a source and a target language, but they should also immerse themselves in the legal jargon and culture of both languages. Therefore, not all interpreters are legal interpreters.

Second, the specific language problems of Cameroon courtroom discourse are related to those linguistic elements that obtrude communication between legal professionals and lay-litigants. Among those linguistics elements we have, the legal jargon, the misinterpretation of terms, the question type, and linguistic bravado.

The Question Types

Questions constitute the principal feature of court examination (Holt & Johnson, 2010). During hearings and before verdicts, lawyers and magistrates examine and cross-examine litigants to obtain evidence of guilt or innocence. This book and other literature accredited the syntactic and semantic complexity of questions. There are different question types (yes or no questions, WH questions, etc.), and the syntactic and semantic structure of questions is often difficult to deconstruct. The syntactic structure of a question can either simplify or make ambiguous its semantic. A hearer capacity to define the semantic of a complex question is linked to his/her proficiency in the target language. Therefore, in courtrooms, one of the first hurdles a lay-litigant must overcome is the identification of the semantic of questions. It often happens that lay-litigants fail to understand legal authorities' questions as demonstrated in cases 1, 2, 20, and 21 of the observation guides. However, Holt and Johnson (2010) proposed some simple question types that could be used by legal professionals in court to avoid ambiguity, And- and So-prefaced questions, Formulations, and Repeating questions.

The Legal Jargon

Legal terminology refers to words that are specific to the legal profession. The legal jargon originated within the legal system to communicate. Vijay (2010) argued that legal discourse is different from most other professional talks in that it is very much dependent on context and text (legal texts). The ramification of the legal jargon makes it difficult to understand, especially for novices (litigants). Lay-litigants' violation of the speech act Felicity conditions was an after-effect of the legal jargon. To ease communication between litigants and legal professionals in legal contexts, Vijay (2010) proposed four rules: clarity, precision, unambiguity, and inclusiveness.

(a) Clarity: Legal terms need to be defined. To accommodate non-legal professionals, professionals may use descriptive sentence. For instance, instead of saying, *do you have a witness*? A judge may say, *do you have a person who saw the event*?
(b) Precision. This necessitates simple sentences rather than complex or compound-complex sentences.
(c) Unambiguity. This implies the certainty of legal words and expressions. Unambiguity is often achieved when using simple words and sentences.
(d) Inclusiveness. This rule involves the principle of 'adequacy of specification of legal scope'. To reach the adequacy of the specification of legal scope, legal texts should strive to attain two objectives: accessibility and transparency. Legal writings should be transparent and accessible. They should not only serve the interest of legal authorities.

However, it does not suffice to clarify or to simplify legal talk to solve the language problems of lay-litigants. Cameroon lay-litigant language problems not only are limited to the legal jargon but also concern the language of use. English and French are not spoken by 40% of the adult population. Therefore, the legal language policy needs to be revised.

Court Interpreting

There is a general tendency to underestimate the task and role of interpreters in courtrooms. People fail to understand that court interpretation is a highly specialised activity. For instance, in Cameroon, no concrete step has ever been taken to provide court interpreters with the necessary skills. This is why, in Chap. 3, we observed the limits and mistakes of interpreters performing in courtrooms. Those shortcomings affect courtroom discourse negatively. For a legal interpretation to be efficient, several conditions must be respected.

One of the first prerequisites in interpretation is a native or native-like control of at least two languages. A second condition is to distinguish semantic from pragmatic. A good interpreter will not only interpret the meaning of a sentence but will also interpreter its context (the cultural implication of a sentence). Court interpreters should also overcome cross-linguistic differences between languages. Example of cross-linguistic differences is tense, gender, and number. In some languages, the marking of tense, gender, and number is crucial, whereas in other languages those elements are irrelevant. It demands much skill to interpret from a language having no gender or tense markers to a language having them; an untrained interpreter would hardly do that.

Also, court interpreters should understand the component of translation. One component of legal translation is legal jargon. Studies demonstrated that bilinguals hardly possess rich legal vocabularies. Another layer of complexity in legal interpretation is the translation of questions. The form and the words used in questions can influence the answers they elicit, and even the recollections they trigger in eyewitnesses (Hale, 2010). Untrained interpreters do not always understand the role and duties of an interpreter in courts. This is the reason why in case 23 of the observation guide, the interpreter whispered his translation in the ears of the judge. Other works showed court interpreters mistakenly correcting, commenting, or advising participants. On the other hand, 'well-trained court interpreter will have the expertise to intervene to explain situations where potential misunderstandings may arise, where direct equivalents are not possible, or where a linguistic strategy does not have the same effect in the target language (Hale, 2010).

Even though the scope of this research was limited to courtroom discourse analysis. I deem it necessary to recognise that it is not the only legal setting that requires FL research in Cameroon. In the following paragraphs, I outline other legal settings that need linguistics and/or Forensic Linguistic investigations.

Police Interviews in Cameroon

All judicial proceedings start with police interviews. The trials that follow police interviews rely on the memos of the officers. Therefore, it is crucial to have a good police interview to have a good and fair trial. But the data demonstrated many litigants complaining about the methods of investigation of officers. For instance, in case 3 of the observation guide, the accused person refuted the veracity of the evidence gotten from the police interview. Indeed, there is a need to study the discourse strategies between the officers and the litigants.

State Counsel's Investigations

The state counsel's investigation follows the interviews of the police officers. Before the start of the trial, the state counsel needs to know the case. In their investigations, state counsels examine (interview) litigants. Just like police interviews, state counsel's investigations also impact trials. Therefore, this step of the judicial proceeding has to be studied to determine the language difficulties lay-litigants encounter.

Lawyers' and Clients' Discourse

Before trials, litigants having the means to pay the services of a lawyer are briefed on what to say and what not to say. Trial examinations and cross-examinations are very stressful; few litigants sustain the pressure. In case 21 of the observation guide, a plaintiff admitted having evidence he never had, and in case 22, an accused person contradicted his lawyer. For sure, scholars need to investigate this domain of law to determine how well lawyers prepare their clients before trials and in which languages it is done.

Cameroon Court Interpreters

Even though I made mention of this domain in the present study, I did not elaborate on the discussion. My point of focus was on lay-litigants' discourse. Besides, I recorded very few court interpretations. However, the collected data allows me to argue that Cameroon court interpreters are not trained and they make many mistakes. Nevertheless, a more elaborated study on the subject matter can bring in more information.

In sum, this chapter summarises the results of the study, proposes linguistic solutions to the language-related problems of Cameroon courtrooms, and presents other domains of studies. Yet, I will not pretend to have outlined and describe all the language issues of Cameroon courtroom discourse. But I hope to have enlightened readers on the linguistic situation of Cameroon courtrooms. And most importantly, I hope that this study will prompt other African linguists to study the linguistic situation of African legal systems.

References

Essono, J.-M. (2001). Le Cameroun et ses langues. In J.-M. Essono (Ed.), *Cameroun: Politique, langues, économie et santé* (pp. 61–87). L'Harmattan.

Hale, S. (2010). Court interpreting: The need to raise the bar—Court interpreters as specialized experts. In C. Malcolm & J. Alison (Eds.), *The Routledge handbook of forensic linguistics* (pp. 440–455). Routledge.

Holt, E., & Johnson, A. (2010). Legal talk: Socio-pragmatic aspects of legal talk—Police interviews and trial discourse. In M. Coulthard & A. Johnson (Eds.), *The Routledge handbook of forensic linguistics* (pp. 21–37). Routledge.

Vijay, K. B. (2010). Legal writing: Specificity specification in legislative writing—Accessibility, transparency, power and control. In M. Coulthard & A. Johnson (Eds.), *The Routledge handbook of forensic linguistics* (pp. 37–51). Routledge.

References

Ainsworth, J. (2010). Miranda right: Curtailing coercion in police interrogation—The failed promise of Miranda v. Arizona. In C. Malcolm & J. Alison (Eds.), *The Routledge handbook of forensic linguistics* (pp. 111–126). Routledge.

Aldridge, M. (2010). Vulnerable witnesses: Vulnerable witnesses in the Criminal Justice System. In C. Malcolm & J. Alison (Eds.), *The Routledge handbook of forensic linguistics* (pp. 296–314). Routledge.

Allard, F. (2001). *The Supreme Court of Canada and its impact on the expression of bijuralism*. Supreme Court of Canada.

Anchang, C. M. (2016, November 9). The advocate, the magistrate/judge and the court registrar. Retrieved from Onambele, Anchang & Associates. http://oaalawpartners@gmail.com

Anyangwe, C. (1987). *The Cameroonian judicial system*. CEPER.

Apprendre le droit. (2017, October 30). *What is the difference between common law and civil law?* Retrieved from http://www.apprendre-le-droit.fr/

Aspers, P., & Corte, U. (2019). What is qualitative in qualitative research. *Qualitative Sociology, 42*, 139–160. https://doi.org/10.1007/s11133-019-9413-7

Atindogbé, G. G., & Dissake, K. M. E. (2019). Forensic linguistics as a tool for the development of Cameroon national languages. *African Study Monographs, 40*(1), 23–44. https://doi.org/10.14989/243208

Austin, J. L. (1962). *How to do things with words*. Oxford University Press.

Bastarache, M. J. (2000). *Bijuralism and the judicial function*. Supreme Court of Canada.

E. M. K. Dissake, *Language and Legal Proceedings*,
https://doi.org/10.1007/978-3-030-76349-7

Bernard, R. H. (2006). *Research methods in anthropology: Qualitative and quantitative approaches* (4th ed.). AltaMira Press.

Bhatia, V. K. (2017). Interpreting law in socio-pragmatic space. *Semiotica, 2017*(216), 109–130.

Bialystok, E. (2000). Against isolationism: Cognitive perspectives on second language research. In X. Bonch-Bruevich (Ed.), *The past, present, and future of second language research: Selected proceedings of the 2000 second language research forum* (pp. 97–103). Cascadilla Press.

Bogdan, R. C. (1972). *Participant observation in organized settings.* Syracuse University Press.

Bulmer, E. (2017). *What is a constitution? Principles and concepts.* International IDEA.

Burns, R. B. (1997). *An introduction to research method* (2nd ed.). Longman.

Cao, D. (2010). Legal translation: Translating legal language. In C. Malcolm & J. Alison (Eds.), *The Routledge handbook of forensic linguistics* (pp. 78–94). Routledge.

Catford, J. (1995). *A linguistic theory of translation.* Oxford University Press.

Chaemsaithong, K. (2012). Performing self on the witness stand: Stance and relational work in expert witness testimony. *Discourse & Society, 23*(5), 465–486.

Chiatoh, B. A., & Akumbu, W. P. (2014). Enhancing English language studies in Cameroon: The mother tongue perspective. *California Linguistic Notes, 39*(1), 23–47.

Chuanyou, Y. (2012). Appreciate others' beauty as well as one's own: A contrastive multimodal discourse analysis of two courtroom trials. In S. Tomblin, N. MacLeod, R. Sousa-Silva, & M. Coulthard (Eds.), *Proceedings of the international association of forensic linguists' tenth biennial conference* (pp. 73–91). Centre for Forensic Linguistics.

Coleman, L., & Kay, P. (1981). Prototype semantics: The English word lie. *Language, 57*(1), 26–44.

Collins Dictionary. (1979). *Collins dictionary of the English language.* Collins.

Commonwealth of Australia. (2002). *Style manual* (6th ed.). Wiley Australia.

Constitution of the Republic of Cameroon. (1996a). Art. 1(2,3,8).

Constitution of the Republic of Cameroon. (1996b). Art. 2(1).

Constitution of the Republic of Cameroon. (1996c). Art. 3(1).

Constitution of the Republic of Cameroon. (1996d). Art. 31(3).

Cotterill, J. (2002a). 'Just one more time…': Aspects of intertextuality in the trials of O. J. Simpson. In J. Cotterill (Ed.), *Language in the legal process* (pp. 147–161). Palgrave Macmillan.

Cotterill, J. (2002b). *Language in the legal process.* Palgrave Macmillan.

Coulthard, M. (2002). Whose voice is this? Invented and concealed dialogue in written records of verbal evidence produced by the police. In J. Cotterill (Ed.), *Legal language in the process* (pp. 19–33). Palgrave Macmillan.

Coulthard, M., & Johnson, A. (2007). *An introduction to forensic linguistics: Language in evidence*. Routledge.
Coulthard, M., & Johnson, A. (2010). *The Routledge handbook of forensic linguistics*. Routledge.
Criminal Procedure Code of the Republic of Cameroon. (2005a). Art. 3(2).
Criminal Procedure Code of the Republic of Cameroon. (2005b). Art. 170(2).
Criminal Procedure Code of the Republic of Cameroon. (2005c). Art. 417(1–3).
Dame, H. G. (2015). *Common law reasoning and institution*. University of London.
Denzin, N. K., & Lincoln, Y. S. (2005). Introduction. The discipline and practice of qualitative research. In N. K. Denzin & Y. S. Lincoln (Eds.), *The Sage handbook of qualitative research* (pp. 1–32). SAGE Publications.
Di Carlo, P., & Good, J. (2014). What are we trying to preserve? Diversity, change, and ideology at the edge of the Cameroonian Grassfields. In K. A. Peter & S. Julia (Eds.), *Endangered languages: Beliefs and ideologies in language documentation and revitalization* (pp. 231–264). Oxford University Press.
Dissake, K., Endurence, M., & Atindogbé, G. G. (2019). *Deaf education and language-based curriculum: The case of the Buea School for the Deaf.* OAsis, COL's Open Access Repository. http://hdl.handle.net/11599/3431
Dornyei, Z. (2007). *Research methods in applied linguistics: Quantitative, qualitative and mixed methodologies*. Oxford University Press.
Drew, P. (1992). Contested evidence in courtroom cross-examination: The case of a trial for rape. In P. Drew & J. Heritage (Eds.), *Talk at work* (pp. 470–520). Cambridge University Press.
Ebai, E. (2011). Criminal liability of the police in Cameroon: Prospects and challenges. *African Journal of Criminology and Justice Studies, 5*(2), 127–146.
Eberhard, D. M., Simons, G. F., & Fennig, C. D. (Eds.). (2019). *Ethnologue: Languages of the world* (22nd ed.). SIL International. Retrieved from http://www.ethnologue.com
Eggins, S., & Slade, D. (1997). *Analysing casual conversation*. Cassell.
Ehrlich, S. (2010). Rape victims: The discourse of rape trials. In C. Malcolm & J. Alison (Eds.), *The Routledge handbook of forensic linguistics* (pp. 265–280). Routledge.
English, F. (2010). Non-native speakers in detention: Assessing non-native speaking detainees' English language proficiency. In M. Coulthard & A. Johnson (Eds.), *The Routledge handbook of forensic linguistics* (pp. 423–440). Routledge.
Essono, J.-M. (2001). Le Cameroun et ses langues. In J.-M. Essono (Ed.), *Cameroun: Politique, langues, économie et santé* (pp. 61–87). L'Harmattan.
Etsuko, O. (2006). Austin's speech act theory and the speech situation. *Esercizi Filosofici, 1*, 1–14.
Farshad, R., Sani, K. A., & Moghadam, K. (2016). Forensic linguistics in the light of crime investigation. *Pertanika Journals of Social Sciences & Humanities, 24*(1), 375–384. Retrieved from http://www.pertanika.upm.edu.my/

Feh, H. B. (2017). Henry, Samuelson & CO., Cameroon. Retrieved September 11, 2017, from https://www.hg.org/article.asp?id=7155

Fombad, M. C. (2007). *Cameroon introductory notes.* University of Pretoria. Pretoria: www.icla.up.ac.za › images › cameroon_country_report.

Fombad, M. C. (2015). Managing legal diversity: Cameroonian bijuralism at a critical crossroad. In V. P. Vernon, Y. M. Mohamed, & A. Koppel (Eds.), *Mixed legal systems, East and West* (pp. 101–119). Ashgate.

French, P. (1994). An overview of forensic phonetics with particular reference to speaker identification. *Forensic Linguistics, 1*(2), 169–181.

Gardinier, D. E. (1963). *Cameroon–United Nations challenge to French policy.* Oxford University Press.

Garner, B. A., & Black, H. C. (2009). *Black's law dictionary* (9th ed.). West.

Glasser, B. G., & Strauss, A. L. (1967). *The discovery of grounded theory: Strategies for qualitative research.* Aldine.

Goffman, E. (1981). *Forms of talk.* Blackwell.

Goodwin, J., & Horowitz, R. (2002). Introduction. The methodological strengths and dilemmas of qualitative sociology. *Qualitative Sociology, 25*(1), 33–47.

Greenberg, J. H. (1963). *The languages of Africa.* Indiana University Press.

Groot, G. R. (2003). *Language and law.* Maastricht University Press.

Gumperz, J. (1982a). *Discourse strategies.* Cambridge University Press.

Gumperz, J. (1982b). *Language and social identity.* Cambridge University Press.

Gumperz, J. (2001). Interactional sociolinguistics: A personal perspective. In D. Schiffrin, D. Tannen, & E. Hamilton (Eds.), *The handbook of discourse analysis* (pp. 220–250). Blackwell.

Hale, S. (2010). Court interpreting: The need to raise the bar—Court interpreters as specialized experts. In C. Malcolm & J. Alison (Eds.), *The Routledge handbook of forensic linguistics* (pp. 440–455). Routledge.

Halliday, M. A. (1973). Explorations in the functions of language. *Journal of Linguistics, 3,* 177–198.

He, X., & Feng, Y. (2016). Mismatched discourses in the petition of Chinese courts. *Law & Social Inquiry, 41*(1), 212–241.

Hibbitts, B. J. (1995). Making motions: The embodiment of law in gesture. *Journal of Contemporary Legal Issues, 51,* 51–82.

Hlophe, J. M. (2000). Official languages and the courts. *South African Law Journal, 117*(4), 690–696.

Holt, E., & Johnson, A. (2010). Legal talk: Socio-pragmatic aspects of legal talk—Police interviews and trial discourse. In M. Coulthard & A. Johnson (Eds.), *The Routledge handbook of forensic linguistics* (pp. 21–37). Routledge.

Jannedy, S., & Mendoza-Denton, N. (2006). Structuring information through gesture and intonation. *Interdisciplinary Studies on Information Structure, 3,* 199–244.

Johnson, A. (2002). So...?: Pragmatic implications of so-prefaced questions in formal police interviews. In J. Cotterill (Ed.), *Language in the legal process* (pp. 91–110). Palgrave Macmillan.

Jürgen, J. (2011). Interaction sociolinguistics and discourse analysis. In J. P. Gee & M. Handford (Eds.), *The Routledge handbook of discourse analysis* (pp. 135–146). Routledge.

Kaschula, H. R., Docrat, Z., & de Vries, A. (2020, April 16). *Why using just one language in South Africa's courts is a problem*. Retrieved from The Conversation: https://theconversation.com/why-using-just-one-language-in-south-africas-courts-is-a-problem-134911

Kiye, M. E. (2015). Conflict between customary law and human rights in Cameroon: The role of the courts in fostering an equitably gendered society. *African Study Monographs, 36*(2), 75–100.

Kristeva, J. (1980). Word, dialogue and novel. In L. S. Roudiez (Ed.), *Desire in language: A semiotic approach to literature and art* (pp. 64–91). Colombia University Press.

Kumar, R. (2011). *Research methodology: A step by step guide for beginners* (3rd ed.). Sage.

Lerner, H. (2006). *Principles of constitutional design*. Cambridge University Press.

Linfoot, K. (2007). *Forensic linguistics, first-contact police interviews, and basic officer training* (PhD dissertation). University of Florida, Florida.

Lubbe, H. J. (2008). *The right to language in court: A language right or a communication right?* University of the Free State.

Madumetsa, K. C. (2010). *Law and language: Solution for multilingual societies*. University of Venda.

Martin, A. E. (2003). *A dictionary of law* (5th ed.). Oxford University Press.

Mathew, D. M., & Mark, T. (2013). Concepts of law. *Southern California Law Review, 86*(517), 517–570.

Matoesian, G. M. (2008). You might win the battle but lose the war: Multimodal, interactive, and extralinguistic aspects of witness resistance. *Journal of English Linguistics, 36*(3), 195–218.

Matoesian, G. (2010). Multimodality and forensic linguistics: Multimodal aspects of victim's narrative in direct examination. In M. Coulthard & A. Johnson (Eds.), *The Routledge handbook of forensic linguistics* (pp. 541–557). Routledge.

Mazeland, H. (2006). Conversation analysis. In B. Keith (Ed.), *Encyclopedia of language & linguistics* (2nd ed., pp. 153–163). Elsevier.

McCarthy, M., Matthiessen, C., & Slade, D. (2010). Discourse analysis. In N. Schmitt (Ed.), *An introduction to applied linguistics* (pp. 53–70). Hodder Education.

McMenamin, R. G. (2002). *Forensic linguistics: Advances in forensic stylistics*. CRC Press.

McMenamin, R. G. (2010). Forensic stylistics: Theory and practice of forensic stylistics. In C. Malcolm & J. Alison (Eds.), *The Routledge handbook of forensic linguistics* (pp. 487–508). Routledge.

Melinkoff, D. (1963). *The language of the law*. Little Brown.

Minium, E. W. (1978). *Statistical reasoning in psychology and education* (2nd ed.). Wiley.

Moeketsi, R. H. (1998). Statements about Sesotho questions used in the South African courtroom. *South African Journal of African Languages, 18*(3), 72–77.

Moeketsi, R. H. (1999a). Discourse structure in a criminal trial of a magistrate's court. *South African Journal of African Languages, 19*, 30–38.

Moeketsi, R. H. (1999b). Some observations on answers to courtroom questions. *South African Journal of African Languages, 19*, 237–244.

Moffatt, S. (2015). Contextualizing scientific research methodologies. *Journal of Research & Method in Education, 5*(6), 52–57.

MOGP. (1992). *The memorandum of good practice on video recorded interviews.* The Home Office.

Monette, D. R., Thomas, J. S., & Cornell, R. D. (1986). *Applied social research to human services.* Holt, Rinehart, and Winston.

Moser, C., & Graham, K. (1989). *Survey methods in social investigation* (2nd ed.). Gower.

Naerssen, V. M. (2012). Faked or truthful second language proficiency: Assessing claims. In S. Tomblin, N. MacLeod, R. Sousa-Silva, & M. Coulthard (Eds.), *Proceedings of the international association of forensic linguists' tenth biennial conference* (pp. 306–314). Centre for Forensic Linguistics.

Nico, H. (2015). The Cameroon penal code. Retrieved from http://hallelaw.com/wp-content/uploads/2015/03/THE-CAMEROON-PENAL-CODE.pdf

Palmer, V. V. (2001). *Mixed jurisdictions worldwide: The third legal family.* Cambridge University Press.

Ralarala, K. M., Kaschula, H. R., & Heydon, G. (Eds.). (2019). *New frontiers in forensic linguistics: Themes and perspectives in language and the law in Africa and beyond.* African Sun Media.

Robert, A. L. (2005). Forensic linguistics: Applying the scientific principles of language analysis to issues of the law. *International Journal of the Humanities, 3*, 1–6.

Rosendal, T. (2008). *Multilingual Cameroon: Policy, practice, problems and solutions.* Gothenburg Africana Informal Series.

Rudin, H. R. (1938). *The Germans in the Cameroons 1884–1914: A case study in modern imperialism.* Yale University Press.

Searle, J. (1969). *Speech acts: An essay in the philosophy of language.* Cambridge University Press.

Searle, J. (1975). Indirect speech acts. In C. Peter & J. L. Morgan (Eds.), *Syntax and semantics* (pp. 59–82). Academic Press.

Selltiz, J., Morton, D., & Stuart, C. (1962). *Research methods in social relations.* Holt, Rinehart and Winston.

Shuy, W. R. (1981). Can linguistic evidence build on defense theory in a criminal case? *Studia Linguistica, 35*(2), 33–49.

Shuy, W. R. (2001a). DARE's role in linguistic profiling. *Dictionary of American Regional English Newsletter*, 00–10. Retrieved from https://dare.wisc.edu/dare-newsletters/

Shuy, W. R. (2001b). Discourse analysis in the legal context. In D. Schiffrin, D. Tannen, & H. Hamilton (Eds.), *The handbook of discourse analysis* (pp. 437–452). Blackwell.

Shuy, W. R. (2002a). Breaking into language and the law: The trial of the insider linguist. In E. J. Alatis, E. H. Hamilton, & A.-H. Tan (Eds.), *Linguistics, language, and the professions: Education, journalism, law, medicine, and technology* (pp. 67–80). Georgetown University Press.

Shuy, W. R. (2002b). To testify or not to testify. In J. Cotterill (Ed.), *Language in the legal process* (pp. 03–18). Palgrave Macmillan.

Shuy, W. R. (2006). *Linguistics in the courtroom: A practical guide.* Oxford University Press.

Simons, G. F., & Fennig, C. D. (Eds.). (2017). *Ethnologue: Language of the world* (20th ed.). SIL International. Retrieved from http://www.ethnologue.com

Smith, H. W. (1991). *Strategies of social research* (3rd ed.). Holt, Rinehart and Winston.

Solan, L. M. (1998). Linguistic experts as semantic tour guides. *Forensic Linguistics, 2*, 87–106.

Solan, L. (1999). Can the legal system use experts on meaning (reprinted in 49 Def. L.J. 775 (2000)).

Solan, L. M. (2002). The Clinton scandal: Some legal lessons from linguistics. In J. Cotterill (Ed.), *Language in the legal process* (pp. 180–195). Macmillan.

Solan, L. M. (2010). The forensic linguist: The expert linguist meets the adversarial system. In C. Malcolm & J. Alison (Eds.), *The Routledge handbook of forensic linguistics* (pp. 395–410). Routledge.

Stygall, G. (2010). Legal writing: Complexity complex documents/average and not-so-average readers. In M. Coulthard & A. Johnson (Eds.), *The Routledge handbook of forensic linguistics* (pp. 51–65). Routledge.

Tetley, W. (2000). Mixed jurisdictions: Common law vs civil law (codified and uncodified). 60 La. L. Rev. Available at: https://digitalcommons.law.lsu.edu/lalrev/vol60/iss3/2

The European Judicial Training Network. (2012). *Language training on the vocabulary of judicial cooperation in criminal matters.* European Judicial Training Network.

The Justice and Peace Commission Archdiocese of Bamenda. (2019). *The judicial system in Cameroon.* Retrieved from https://www.justiceandpeacebamenda.org/attachments/article/24/The+Judicial+System+in+Cameroon.pdf

Thyer, B. A. (1993). Single-systems research design. In R. M. Grinnell (Ed.), *Social work research and evaluation* (4th ed., pp. 94–117). Peacock.

Tiersma, M. P. (2002). The language and law of product warnings. In J. Cotterill (Ed.), *Language in the legal process* (pp. 54–72). Palgrave Macmillan.

Tomblin, S., MacLeod, N., Rui, S.-S., & Coulthard, M. (2012). *Proceedings of the international association of forensic linguists' tenth biennial conference* (pp. 1–368). Centre for Forensic Linguistics, Aston University.

Tschonghongei, N. C. (2012). *Juridical lexicon and translation pragmatics in Aghem* (Unpublished master's thesis). University of Yaoundé I.

Verschueren, J. (1999). *Understanding pragmatics.* Edward Arnold.

Vijay, K. B. (2010). Legal writing: Specificity specification in legislative writing—Accessibility, transparency, power and control. In M. Coulthard & A. Johnson (Eds.), *The Routledge handbook of forensic linguistics* (pp. 37–51). Routledge.

Virbel, J. (2015). Speech act theory and instructional texts. In K. Chemla & J. Virbel (Eds.), *Textual acts and the history of science* (pp. 49–58). Springer.

Wachal, R. S. (1966). *Linguistic evidence, statistical inference and disputed authorship* (Unpublished PhD dissertation). University of Wisconsin, Wisconsin.

Walliman, N. (2011). *Research methods: The basics.* Routledge.

Wilkinson, D., & Birmingham, P. (2003). *Using research instruments: A guide for researchers.* Routledge.

Woodbury, H. (1984). The strategic use of questions in court. *Semiotica, 48*(4), 197–228.

Index[1]

[1] Note: Page numbers followed by 'n' refer to notes.

E. M. K. Dissake, *Language and Legal Proceedings*,
https://doi.org/10.1007/978-3-030-76349-7

The manufacturer's authorised representative in the EU is Springer Nature Customer Service Centre GmbH, Europaplatz 3, 69115 Heidelberg, Germany. If you have any concerns regarding our products, please contact ProductSafety@springernature.com

Printed and bound by CPI Group (UK) Ltd, Croydon, CR0 4YY
30/09/2026
02225466-0008